Home
Tanning
&
Leathercraft
Simplified

Home Tanning & Leathercraft Simplified

BY KATHY KELLOGG

W WILLIAMSON PUBLISHING CO.

CHARLOTTE, VERMONT 05445

Library of Congress Cataloging in Publication Data

Kellogg, Kathy.
    Home tanning & leathercraft simplified.

    Bibliography: p.
    1. Tanning—Amateurs' manuals. 2. Leather work—
Amateurs' manuals. I. Title.
TS985.K39   1984   675'.2   83-26123
ISBN 0-913589-04-7

Cover and interior design: Trezzo-Braren Studio
Illustrations: Loretta Trezzo
Drawings page 112–115: Susan Kraemer
Photographs: Kathleen A. Kellogg
Printing: Capital City Press

Williamson Publishing Co.
P.O. Box 185
Charlotte, Vermont 05445
1-800-234-8791

Manufactured in the United States of America

10

*This book is dedicated to my husband, Bob,
who is always there when I need him
and who never stops believing in me.*

Acknowledgements

Many people helped to make this book possible. First, I'd like to thank Jack Williamson for giving me the opportunity to write it. We both agreed that a complete tanning handbook, up-to-date and easy to understand, was important and needed on the market.

Also, I'd like to thank my family for believing in my project, supporting me during my many hours of research and writing (helping when they could), and forgiving me when dinner was often late and the laundry piled up! Special thanks to my daughter, Melissa, for being my model and to my sister, Susan Kraemer, for her graphic contributions.

I'd also like to extend my gratitude to the following persons for their help: Ruth Price of the U.S.D.A. Office of Governmental & Public Affairs, Photography Division; Loretta Trezzo for her illustrations; Mildred Keefer of Sunrise Meadows Enterprises; John Mitchell from the New England Tanners Club; The Tacoma Tandy Leather Store; Mrs. Gail Sanden of Empress Chinchilla, and Earl Allen from the Fur Takers of America.

contents

Dedication • 5

Acknowledgements • 6

Contents • 7

Introduction • 11

Part I: Skins, Hides & Pelts • 13

    Introduction • 14

    Chapter I: The Fur-bearers • 17

        The Prime Fur-farm Animals • 17

        Wild Fur Trapping • 20

        When to Skin for Prime Fur • 22

        Methods of Killing • 25

        Skinning • 25

        After Skinning • 26

    Chapter 2: Larger Animals • 29

        Killing • 30

        Skinning • 30

        After Skinning • 36

contents

Part II: Tanning • 41

    Introduction • 42
    Tanning Chemicals Overview • 42
    Tanning Variables • 43

      Chapter 3: Tanning for Fur • 47
        Fleshing • 49
        Drying • 52
        Breaking the Skin: Softening • 55
        Drumming • 58
        Other Finishing Steps • 58
        Tanning Recipes • 60
          Alum-Salt • 60
            Immersion Methods, Basic Alum-Salt • 61
            Immersion, Alum-Salt-Soda • 62
            Pasting Methods • 63
          Acid-Salt Methods • 63
            Basic Recipe • 64
        Tanning Tests • 65
        Final Thoughts • 65

      Chapter 4: Tanning for Leather • 67
        Fleshing • 68
        Removing the Hair • 71
        Deliming • 72
        Rawhide • 73
        Tanning • 74
          Chrome Tan • 75
        Finishing • 78
          Coloring • 78
          Thick Leathers (Sole, Harness, Belt) • 78
          Thin Leathers (Garment) • 80

Chapter 5: Other Tanning Methods • 83
   Vegetable Tanning • 83
   Retanning • 88
   Mineral Tanning • 88
      Alum/Washing Soda • 88
      Oxalic Acid • 88
      Carbolic Acid • 89
   Oil Tanning • 90
   Buckskin • 90
      Indian Buckskin • 90
      White Man's Buckskin • 92
   Sheepskin • 92
      Alternative Sheepskin Tanning Methods • 92
      Sheepskin Mats • 93
      Glutaraldehyde Tanning • 93
   Snakeskins & Other Novelty Leathers • 96
      Tanning Snakeskins • 96
      Alligator • 97
      Shark • 97

Chapter 6: Troubleshooting • 99

Part III: Leather and Fur Crafting • 105

Introduction • 106
   Types of Leather • 108
   Hand Sewing • 112
   Machine Sewing • 117

Chapter 7: Elementary Leatherwork • 121
   Tools and Material • 121
   Cutting a Pattern • 124
   Tooling • 126
   Dyeing • 127
   Assembling • 128
      Stitching and Lacing • 128
      Rivets and Snaps • 130
      Gluing • 130
   Project: Leather Belt, Wristband or Collar • 131
   Footwear Primer • 138
   Leather Care • 139
      Suede and Split Leathers • 139
      Smooth and Grained Leather • 139

contents

Chapter 8: Sewing With Fur • 141
    Matching Pelts • 143
    Choosing a Pattern • 144
    Cutting Furskins • 145
    Plugging Holes • 147
    Sewing with Fur • 148
        Hand Sewing • 148
        Seams • 149
        Hems • 149
        Joining Fur to Fabric/Soft Leather • 150
        Easing • 150
        Darts • 150
        Pockets • 151
        Findings • 151
        Lining • 151
    Project: Fur-lined Mittens • 152
    Scraps • 160
    Dyeing Furs and Fur Garments • 160
    Mink Industry Methods • 160
    Felt Manufacture from Rabbit Fur • 162
    Care and Cleaning of Fur Garments & Crafts • 162

Chapter 9: Basic Taxidermy • 165
    Novelty Taxidermy • 168
    Fur Rugs • 170

Appendix • 175
    Glossary • 175
    Suggested Reading/Bibliography • 182
    For More Information • 183
    Fur Buyers • 184
    Leather & Fur Sellers • 185
    Suppliers • 186

Index • 189

introduction

This is a book about an often-ignored but readily available natural resource that you can use to create beautiful, useful garments, footwear, and crafts. This book is about leathers: creating them from hides and skins and using them to make your own leather items.

Leather, with or without the naturally occurring hair or fur, is preserved animal skin. The process of preservation is known as tanning, and it is the oldest craft known to man, his first art.

It was natural for primitive man to use the skins and furs of the animals he hunted. The tanned hides could be used to protect his feet, power a slingshot, and keep him warm in the winter and cool in the summer. Hide use can be traced to the first nomadic hunting and gathering tribes. In fact, according to ancient documents, the Egyptians and Hebrews wore leather clothing at least 5,000 years ago. It was only when man adapted himself to a more settled, domestic lifestyle that he developed additional arts such as pottery, spinning, and weaving.

Leather, then, was man's first clothing material and plays an important, necessary role in human history. The playwright Aristophanes referred to the tanner as an already well-established trade in Athens 500 years before the birth of Christ. America's first tanner, Experience Miller, came to Plymouth and set up business in the colonies barely three years behind the first Pilgrims. But tanning in America dates back to before the European settlers arrived. The American Indians made excellent leathers from deer and elk skins and buffalo hides that they used for their moccasins, garments, and tents.

Today, most leathers and furs are by-products of the meat industry and are processed at massive tanneries using modern equipment. However, the isolated rancher or homesteader as well as the leather craftsperson can still convert hides into leather like the pioneers of yesterday, by hand, without expensive machinery.

To make food production economical it is important to use all the by-products possible, so don't ignore the potential of using hides and skins obtained from meat animals. And, of course, using all the resources available from a butchered animal without wasting even the skins increases your ecological awareness of the patterns and cycles of the earth's precious gifts.

But beyond the economical and ecological justification of tanning and using your own leathers, there is the simple emotional satisfaction you get from perfecting an art and expressing your creativity through an ancient craft.

There are nearly as many ways to tan skins and sew leathers as there are tanners, taxidermists, leatherworkers, and furriers. No one person knows all there is to know about this craft, and there are few, if any, strict rules to follow. My techniques are right for me, but my methods are not the only ones, and what I advise is not final. If you can think of a better way, try it! New ideas and better methods are discovered in every field every day — in fact, this is how progress is made. Success in any art depends largely on the skill of the artist, and the only way to perfect any skill is to practice, practice, practice, and then practice some more.

In this book, I have discussed most of the problems you might encounter, and I have suggested easier, faster, and less expensive ways for the beginner as well as covering traditional, labor-intensive tanning methods. By applying the knowledge you gain from this text and a little common sense of your own, any difficulties you encounter should be relatively easy to overcome.

The main point to remember as you try tanning for the first time or improve your techniques with practice is that it should be fun! You should end up with a glowing sense of pride in your accomplishments as well as a serviceable piece of leather or fur.

part I

Skins, Hides & Pelts

Introduction

Leather comes in a wide variety of types — as many, in fact, as there are animals. The most common leathers are made from cowhide, calfskin, sheepskin, and pigskin. Sheep and calf skins may be commonly tanned with the hair intact. Small fur-bearing skins, such as those from rabbits, mink, and raccoon, are almost always tanned with the fur in place because the leather is generally too thin for use by itself and the fur adds to the warmth and beauty of the finished product.

Traditionally, the tanner refers to the skin coverings of large animals such as cattle, horses, mules, hogs, and others as hides. Those of smaller animals are called skins, and the term pelt is usually reserved for an untanned hide or skin with the hair on or a tanned fur-bearing skin. However, these terms are often used interchangeably by the layman, and they will be used to mean the same thing (the tanned or untanned skin covering of any animal with or without the hair or fur) in this text.

Today, most skins and hides used for leather are by-products of the meat-processing industry, and most fur is obtained from specialized fur farms and trappers. Only 4–5 percent of the larger hides used for leather are obtained from animals butchered on the farm by individual farmers. An even smaller percentage of hides are tanned on the farm. Smaller meat animals (rabbits, calves, young goats, and lambs) are often home-butchered, but the skins of these animals are rarely tanned or even sent out to commercial tanneries. In fact, most are discarded as waste.

Hides for leather are best if taken in the summer and early fall before the skin is depleted of nutrients needed to grow the winter coat of hair. At this time, the hair on the hide is thin and easily removed. A heavy winter coat is best used for rugs and fur. However, keep in mind that a heavy hair coat retains moisture and heat which increases the risk of decay and rot before tanning can begin. Also, when the fur or hair is thick and lush, the leather is thinner.

Most farm butchers and home tanners are not aware that several potentially deadly diseases can be transmitted to man through contact with infected animals, their bedding, and their carcasses and skins. Diseases of this type are anthrax, brucellosis (Bang's disease), bubonic plague, leptospirosis, rabies, Rocky Mountain spotted fever, ringworm, and tularemia. Mange and distemper are two diseases common among trapped wild animals that can be transmitted to domestic animals by unwise handling. (See the glossary in the appendix for a discussion of these diseases including methods of transmission and symptoms.)

Although it is permissible to use the hides from animals that have died of natural causes or in an accident, these skins are generally of lower quality than those taken from healthy animals. Generally, I recommend that you don't even attempt to skin such animals, wild or domestic. Bury, burn, or otherwise dispose of the hide with the carcass. Even though rubber gloves may afford some protection during skinning, the hide will never make quality leather and you always run the risk of accidental infection.

The first two chapters of this book will get you started on how to make animal skin into leather and fur. The first chapter will discuss the small, fur-bearing animals: how to choose for prime fur, how to butcher and skin, and how to avoid losing the pelt to decay and rot before you start tanning. The second chapter will cover the same points in a discussion of larger animals taken generally for leather.

Keep in mind that the value of the hide to you, the tanner, is determined by the quality of the leather it will eventually make. The difference between a good hide and a poor one is measured by your choice of the animal, your skill during skinning, and your care when preparing and preserving the hide.

The New Zealand.

chapter 1

The
Furbearers

The Prime Fur-Farm Animals

The domestic rabbit is perhaps the most popular and readily available species of fur-bearing animal raised in the United States and abroad. This furry creature is raised for its beautiful coat, is a popular meat source, a show animal, and is used in biomedical research.

Rabbits are relatively simple to raise indoors or out, in wooden hutches, all-wire cages, or even in groups on fenced pasture. The females can produce four or more litters each year, each litter averaging six to eight young. Rabbits are butchered for meat between eight and twelve weeks, but animals raised strictly for fur are usually held until six months of age or older. The meat of mature fur animals is no longer prime, but can be roasted, stewed, or used in sausage.

France, Belgium, Italy, and some of the oriental countries produce most of the rabbit furs used by the commercial fur trade.

Four Types

Rabbit fur comes in four basic types and many colors. The common fur is about an inch long and has a fine wool next to the skin with longer guard hairs. Satin fur is also about an inch long, but is intensely colored and lustrous because of the smaller diameter hair shaft and transparent hair shell. Rex fur is perhaps the most important type in the fur industry. It is short (about ½ inch), plush, dense, and soft with guard hairs almost as long as the underfur. Angora fur is more properly known as wool. It is up to three inches long and is harvested several times a year and spun for yarn.

Rabbit skins are easy to tan and sew and are an excellent choice for the beginner. Not only are they fairly simple to find, but they also make some truly beautiful fur garments and craft items.

Raising Mink

Mink are small, temperamental animals that require a great deal of time, energy, money, and efficiency to raise. They have razor-sharp teeth and scent glands similar to skunks, but not as highly developed, and have been known to turn on their handlers. Raising these animals is not a project for the backyard fur-farmer.

The American fur market is influenced by tradition and history to favor domestic ranch mink. Europeans, on the other hand, prefer furs of wild animals such as coyote and fox. Ranch mink is naturally a dark brown but, as a result of intentional mutations, it is available today in twelve basic natural colors ranging from black and white to blue, grey, and even pink. Most wild mink, which are trapped rather than raised, have golden brown fur. Mink are naturally shaded because of the presence of top hair and underfur. In most mink, the darkest fur is along the back, and it gets progressively lighter towards the belly.

It requires about 100 pounds of feed to produce one mink pelt. The females have one litter per year, usually in May from a February to March breeding. The average litter size is three to four kits. The young are weaned at about eight weeks of age and are ready to butcher for prime pelts in early winter when they are six to seven months old. Each mink is put into an individual furring pen for its last month to grow a coat of flawless fur, since mink will fight and damage their pelts if housed together. The fur reaches its peak for only about a ten-day period when it is fluffy, cushiony, and has good color tone. Pelts in prime condition with well-developed guard hairs and underfur are known as full-furred.

Chinchilla

The chinchilla is a small animal resembling a squirrel. It is raised for fur, breeding stock, and biomedical research. It is a vegetarian with

Handling mink requires heavy gloves and a calm
attitude to avoid bites. (U.S.D.A.)

eating and living habits similar to a rabbit, both being nocturnal or most active at night. When startled, it will make a series of quick jumping, hopping movements and can be difficult to control.

Mature animals weigh only one to two pounds. Females produce one to three litters per year (the average is a little over two) with one to six young in each litter. The average is about three.

Chinchilla fur is very fine and silky with white-banded effects and a veiled appearance because the tips of the hair fibers are black. The fur is generally grey with a deep blue-grey underfur, but it may vary from very light to very dark. The fur is usually prime in December to March, and the mature animal will shed this coat in late spring if not harvested.

The pelts of young rabbits, mink, and chinchilla are very small, thin, and fragile, and the utmost care is required during skinning and tanning. If you are a beginner, stick to older (four to six months of age) rabbit skins which are larger, thicker, and more durable.

Other Animals

Several other fur-bearing animals are raised on fur farms. They include the fox, marten, fisher, coypu (nutria), and karakul, a breed of sheep. Wise and careful fur farming helps protect valuable fur species from extinction while providing sufficient fur products to meet the demands of the consumer.

Although not usually considered fur-bearing animals, sheep, lambs, goats, and calves are often raised and butchered on the farm with their hides used as fur skins. As compared to other furbearers who generally have quality pelts for limited times only, the pelts of these larger animals are usually in acceptable tanning condition most of the year. However, when the wool of sheepskins is four inches or longer or if the wool is matted and starting to shed, the skin is not suitable for tanning as a woolskin. For further information about skinning and tanning woolskins and hairhides, see Chapters 2 and 4.

Wild Fur Trapping

Many fur-bearing animals are trapped rather than raised mainly because they cost too much or are too difficult to maintain in captivity. Included are the beaver, seal, muskrat, fitch, skunk, raccoon, opossum, otter, and weasel.

One of the most valuable species of trapped furbearers is the ermine weasel. It is native to northern Russia and Scandinavia, but a re-

A fur trapper with his catch of the season. (U.S.D.A.)

lated species, known as the white weasel, lives in North America. This animal has a brown summer fur coat and a white winter coat above 35° north latitude. The very same animal remains brown the year round south of this latitude.

The H.E. Goldberg Company, a fur buyer in Seattle, Washington, takes in wild furs trapped in Alaska, Canada, Siberia, and the northern United States, mainly for shipment to Europe. Only those furs taken in the winter and fully prime are of high enough quality to command the premium prices paid to the trappers.

When asked why the fur market persists in an age of synthetics and despite the complaints of consumer groups and animal-rights activists, Irwin Goldberg, president of the H.E. Goldberg Co. and son of the founder, explained: "It's a psychological thing. An emotional thing. A touch thing. You cannot produce a substitute that feels like real fur. Once you decide you like furs, you're hooked!"

When to Skin for Prime Fur

Primeness of fur in all species of fur-bearing animals is determined by the fur's texture, density, and condition. Good fur texture is soft and lush without being stiff, wiry, thin, or overly fluffy. Fur density is determined by the amount of underfur and guard hairs; prime pelts have very dense fur. Condition refers to the overall evenness of the fur and the hair height, color, and luster. If a furskin meets all these criteria, it is a top-grade pelt by fur industry standards.

As a general rule, summer furskins are poorly haired and of inferior quality. Further, all fur-bearing animals go through periods of molt or shedding, usually in the spring and the autumn (the guard hairs grow in first and the underfur fills in later). Many, like the mink and the rabbit, are not in tight coat (completely free from molt) for very long, often as short a time as a few days. Because the hair from a molting skin will tend to shed, even after tanning, it is important to choose animals in tight coat when fur quality is important, such as when you are selling commercially. To detect molt in colored breeds, blow into the fur along the spine. A prime skin will be pale flesh or cream colored. Bluish patterns or patches on the skin under the hair (and on the flesh side after skinning) indicates the molting condition due to pigment of the new hair showing through. The presence of dead or short hair and hairs that can be pulled easily from the live animal's skin also indicate molt.

When an animal such as the rabbit is raised for meat and the fur is a secondary resource, the quality of the fur is not as important as the meat, which is best when the animal is between six and fourteen weeks of age. However, skins from rabbits less than nine weeks old are almost too thin for proper handling and useless for making any sort of garment. The best rabbit pelt for producing tanned fur is from a rabbit about six months old that has molted twice and is in its third coat. Nonetheless, skins from young fryers, molting fryers, and older cull or roaster rabbits can be used for some projects, and, at worst, they are excellent for practice.

Getting Prime Skins

Whether you are raising rabbits and other furbearers for meat or for fur, following a few common-sense rules will assure that the fur you obtain is as prime as it can be. Poor environmental conditions will produce rabbits or any other caged fur animals with poor quality pelts. For instance, overcrowding the young animals will result in fighting and fur-chewing, and urine-stained fur. Cages placed too close together or

The Californian is a common meat type also used for fur. (U.S.D.A.)

having solid or dirty floors will also tend to produce furs with brownish or yellow urine stains. There is no way to remove urine stains or repair the damage from fighting, The best way is to avoid them. Good nutrition, clean drinking water, and disease prevention will all help to avoid problems.

Although most land furbearers have prime furs in winter, aquatic animals usually have the best fur in early to mid spring when the waters are the coldest from melting snow. Hence, when rabbits and mink are starting to molt in April and May, the coats of the river-dwelling otter and beaver are in prime condition.

Now you should have a good idea of when to butcher—when the animal's coat is thick, lush, soft, and does not shed. The next question is how.

Various stages of a rabbit butcher.

Methods of Killing

Try to kill the animal as quickly and as painlessly as possible, for the sake of both the animal and the butcher.

Humane death and merciful killing methods are important to modern trappers. Says Major L. Boddicker of The Fur Takers of America, "Trapping devices were and are needed to catch and hold animals . . . since other means do not efficiently take them. We use the most humane traps that 20,000 years of experience have developed. The pain or suffering an animal might experience in a trap prior to a humane death would be an unfortunate accident in the process."

Trappers try to insure a quick death by the action of the trap, a drowning device, or with other humane methods. Animals that could injure the trapper, such as bobcats, badgers, and raccoons, are shot with a .22 rifle either through the spine between the shoulder blades, directly in the heart or lungs through the chest, or through the spine of the neck. Other smaller animals such as muskrats and opossums may be killed by a sharp blow to the base of the skull. Some animals are caught in a box trap and safely, cleanly drowned by submerging the entire trap. Care should be taken when moving the trap, especially if it contains a scent-producer like a skunk.

Trappers try to utilize the meat and other by-products from trapped furbearers as baits, lures, dog and cat foods, and even for human consumption. Many have excellent taste and texture, and a high nutritional value.

Farm-raised furbearers are usually killed with carbon monoxide gas, electric shock, lethal injection, or a quick blow to the head. Some rabbit-raisers suggest killing by dislocating the neck. I have never been able to master this technique and have found a blow to the forehead with a hammer or club faster and easier.

In either case, keep in mind the two main objectives: quick and painless.

Skinning

Remove the skin from the animal while the carcass is still warm as it separates more easily at this stage. Most furbearers are butchered while hanging from one or both hind feet by hooks or ropes.

Small animals should be skinned by beginning at one of the hind feet and slitting the skin down to the anus. Cut carefully around this area, avoiding any scent glands. These look like large bumps on either side of the anus/vent region. Don't cut into them or put too much pressure on these areas when loosening the skin. Then cut up to the other foot. Peel the skin off the hind legs and carcass by drawing it wrong side out over the body, fur side in, like removing a glove. Loosen the tight spots with your fingers. Resort to a sharp skinning knife only when absolutely necessary (see Chapter 2 for a complete discussion of skinning knives). Such an uncut pelt is called *cased* or *sleeve-pulled.*

Some furskins such as those of mature, male rabbits, wolves, coyotes, and other larger wild animals must be skinned open in a way similar to cattle and sheep (see Chapter 2). This method requires the hide to be slit from anus to throat along the belly line and the skin gradually loosened with a sharp knife and the fingers.

After Skinning

Fresh skin will begin to decay a few hours after flaying or skinning, just as meat will spoil, unless steps are taken to prevent it. Pelts must be cooled quickly and thoroughly because body heat will cause a skin to spoil faster than artificial heat. Such spoilage results in a condition known as *hairslip* (see Chapter 5 for a full discussion), and once the hairs have begun to slip on an animal skin, there is little chance to save it.

One way to cool the skin is to slice the cased pelt up the belly line, then spread it out in a cool place for thirty minutes or more. Uncut pelts may be cooled on wire stretcher racks designed for this purpose. Another method is to submerse the fresh hide in ice-cold water for several minutes.

Unless you intend to tan the skin immediately after cooling, it must be preserved by freezing (wrap to prevent dehydration), drying, or curing with salt. Most fur buyers prefer to purchase uncut cased pelts, cooled, and dried on wire stretchers.

Occasionally you will find an extremely greasy pelt, particularly those of raccoons, sheep, and water-dwellers such as beaver. After cooling it thoroughly, you can degrease such a skin by washing it with soap or detergent after scraping off as much fat as possible. Rinse thoroughly, as any soap left in the pelt will interfere with tanning. If the skin is still greasy, wash it thoroughly in gasoline and then again in soap and water.

Except for removing grease or excessive dirt, washing a skin before tanning is usually unnecessary. After the tanning process is complete, the pelt is washed and rinsed before drying anyway.

When the cooling is completed, you are ready to begin tanning (see Chapter 3).

Cased (uncut) rabbit pelts and some wrapped
for the freezer in plastic freezer bags.

chapter 2

Larger Animals

Several common domestic and wild animals provide skins for tanning into leather. Generally, the hair is removed from these hides before tanning (see Chapter 4).

Cowhides are perhaps the most common and readily available skins used in the leather industry and are generally a by-product of the beef industry. Horsehide is similar in weight and thickness to cowhide, and both types produce a leather that is heavy and thick and used for shoe soles, belts, and harnesses. Hides from mature cattle and horses weigh sixty or more pounds and are forty square feet or larger in size. Hides this large are usually cut into two or more pieces for ease of handling when tanning.

Medium-sized skins, often called *kips*, include those of calves, goats, sheep, and deer. These skins are sometimes prepared with the hair intact, but usually it is removed as with larger hides to produce a light, thin, supple leather used for garments and gloves. Skins from calves, horses, and sheared sheep or goats that are six to eight months old weigh about eight to fifteen pounds and are seven to ten square feet in size. They are usually tanned in one piece, although they may be sectioned like cowhide.

Pigskin is another common hide, originally used for footballs. It is tough and durable. However, most domestic hogs are not skinned but the hair is removed in scalding during butchering. The hides from these animals would make a poor leather because the hair pores often pierce entirely through the skin, right into the fat layer.

Although you will probably never be faced with a hide larger than a bearskin (which is usually treated like a large furskin), just consider the fresh skin of an elephant. It may weight as much as 2,500 pounds and be up to 2½ inches thick. As you can probably guess, larger is always more complicated, and this large is almost impossible. Whenever you are butchering an animal larger than a goat or tanning a hide larger than a sheepskin, consider the advantages of having one or more helpers. Trying to do it all yourself will most likely result in an unsatisfactory product for your intensive effort.

Killing

Your goal should be to kill the animal as quickly and humanely as possible and in a manner that will insure thorough blood drainage. Beef animals are usually knocked out with a stunning hammer or shot with a .22 caliber rifle at a point midway between the ears and slightly above the eye level on the forehead. Stunning is preferable to shooting for more efficient bleeding.

If you can't bear to look the animal in the eyes while killing it, you can shoot it a few inches from the back of the head at such an angle that the bullet lodges in the brain, or give it a sharp blow to the back of the head with a heavy hammer.

Avoid any damage to the hide or the carcass during the killing and handling of the animal. Remember, too, that thirsty, excited, overheated animals will be twice as hard to skin, so keep the animal calm and cool. If it is dirty, give it a scrub, and save yourself some difficult work later.

Skinning

The carcass should be skinned while it is still warm, as the hide is easier to remove at this point. Skinning requires skill that only comes from practice and a great deal of patience to assure that the leather produced will not be marred with cuts and scores caused by negligence or trying to do the job too fast.

Medium-sized and small animals can be hoisted from a strong tree limb or other support so that the carcass clears the ground by a foot or more. All skinning can be accomplished from this position.

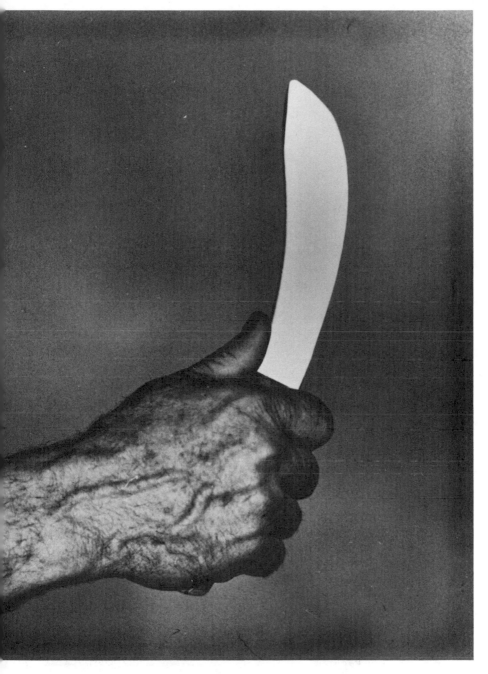

The proper way to hold a skinning knife. (U.S.D.A.)

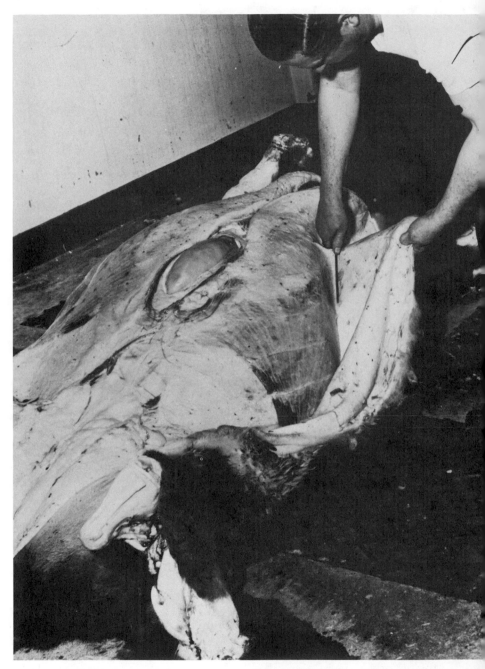

Siding. (U.S.D.A.)

Large animals such as mature cattle are usually partially skinned while on the ground, then hoisted up, often with the aid of block and tackle, and the skinning is completed.

Skinning knives are the most important tool you will need for the skinning operation, and a good job cannot be accomplished without one. They should have well-rounded ends and curved edges to help prevent nicking or cutting the hide, and you should use a steel to keep them very sharp all during the skinning process. Use these knives for no other purpose than skinning and they will stay sharp and useful.

Look for skinning knives that have ⅛-inch thick, heavy steel blades, and be sure that the entire blade from point to heel is equally sharp.

Except when making opening cuts, the knife should be held as in the illustration, with the thumb resting on the back of the blade. Use the knife as little as you can. In many places, the hide can be separated from the carcass with a little gentle tugging or a few blows from your fist. The more you depend on the skinning knife, the greater your chances of cuts and scores.

Draining

The first step is called *sticking* and refers to the process of cutting the animal's throat to allow for complete blood drainage. Do NOT cut crosswise through the hide at the throat. Instead, use a straight slash in line with the center of the underlip and the center of the chest. If you are inexperienced, make the cut about a foot long and deep enough to expose the windpipe. Next, cut the throat crosswise *under* the skin. Make sure that the blood can drain away from the carcass. Don't leave it lying in a pool of blood.

The alternative to sticking is removing the entire head, as is usually done with smaller animals, especially if the hide on the head isn't valuable.

As soon as bleeding has been completed, skin out the forelegs and the head and remove them. With smaller animals, remove the head and cut off the legs at the first joint above the feet.

Cutting Hide

The next step is to cut the hide from chin to base of tail along the center of the belly. The all-important pattern of the hide (the portions that are shoulder, belly, and butt sections) is governed by this initial cut and the cuts to the legs. Be careful and exact. The cut must be straight, even, and without ragged edges. Don't make the leg cuts until you have skinned out the sides or those cuts will be uneven and jagged.

Siding is the process of loosening the skin from the abdomen. It is extremely difficult to do a good job at this stage if you hurry. Start in at about the middle of the belly and work forward toward the head and then back close to the tail. Leave the hide attached to the thighs and shoulders, but loosen the belly skin from the flesh with sweeping knife strokes while pulling the skin away with your other hand. Keep the hide taut and free of wrinkles. Try to loosen the hide to within six or eight inches of the backbone on both sides. You might try beating off the hide with your fist or a dull hatchet instead of relying on the skinning knife. This often results in a better appearance of the carcass and less damage to the hide.

Next, cut down the inside of each leg from the first joint to the belly cut. The foreleg cuts should meet at a point forward, toward the head, of where the legs meet the body. The hind legs' cuts meet at a point about eight inches from the root of the tail.

The "siding," or cutting in half, of a cattle hide.
(The New England Tanners' Club)

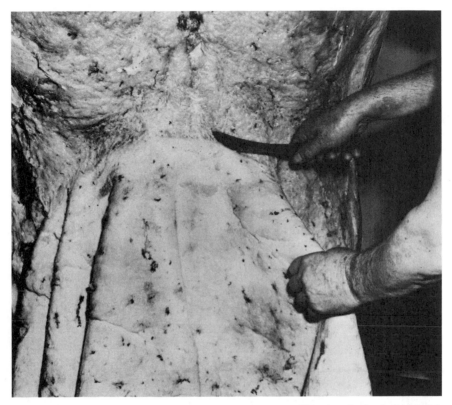

Skinning the back. (U.S.D.A.)

The next step, called *rumping*, is removing the hide from the buttocks and rump. The hide can sometimes be removed by grasping the loose skin and pulling down. Although the hide over the hindquarters is the most valuable, it also tends to be the tightest section and requires slow, careful work to remove without damaging by cuts, nicks, and scrapes. Hence, work as much as you can with your fingers and fists, and rely on the skinning knife as little as possible.

Finally, remove the skin from the back along the backbone.

Use Fingers

Young animals, like calves, skin out much easier than mature ones and most of the hide can be worked off with the fingers.

Leave the *fell* (the thin membrane that lies between the skin and the meat) and as much fat as possible on the carcass to help protect the meat.

When skinning an animal like a bear or wolf for use as a fur rug with feet, you, of course, must not remove the feet when starting the skinning process. Instead, cut through the center of the pad or paw and disjoint at the first joint of the toes, leaving the claws attached to the skin. If you want to leave the head on your rug, skinning is very difficult and requires meticulous work. Follow the directions in one of the excellent taxidermy manuals listed in the Appendix.

The Greeks have an interesting way to remove the hide from a goat. They blow it up like a balloon through a small incision in the skin between the hind legs. You can accomplish the same thing by using a hand-operated tire pump or even a hose and cold water. The cold water method has another benefit in that it cools the hide and the meat during removal. A lamb can be skinned in basically the same way.

After Skinning

Cool the green hide for six to eight hours on a concrete floor or on poles until all the body heat has dissipated. Sheepskins take somewhat longer, as the wool tends to hold the body heat. While the hide is cooling, flesh side up, scrape off as much flesh and fat as you can and trim away any irregular or ragged edges and any parts containing large holes.

If you are not going to tan the skin immediately, it must be cured (treated with salt) to prevent decay. In warm weather, especially, this must be done on the same day as skinning. Salt penetration is better when curing is done as soon as possible after the skin has cooled to room temperature. Large hides, such as those from cattle and horses, are often easier to work with if split into two or more sections (see illustration for the standard cuts and names). In the leather industry, cattle hides are split into four strips—two backs and two bellies—with the back strips being thicker and more valuable.

Before curing, wash the skin or strips with a brush and water to remove dirt, blood and manure.

Applying Salt

Spread the clean, cooled hide in a cool, dry place with the flesh side up and preferably on a slant. A sheet of plywood propped up on one end works well. Apply non-iodized salt, coarse canning-type for thick hides and finer, table-type for thin ones, to every inch of the skin. Use at least ½ to 1 pound per pound of hide. That's a lot, but you need that much to preserve the hide from decay. The salt will dissolve in the

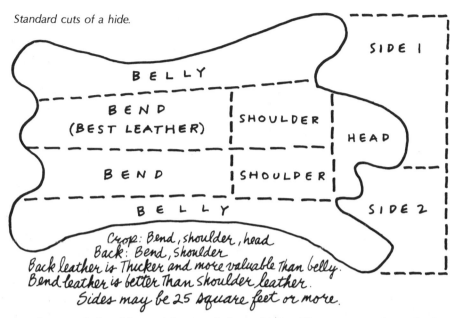

Standard cuts of a hide.

BELLY

BEND
(BEST LEATHER)

SHOULDER

HEAD

BEND

SHOULDER

BELLY

SIDE 1

SIDE 2

Crop: Bend, shoulder, head
Back: Bend, shoulder
Back leather is Thicker and more valuable Than belly.
Bend leather is better Than shoulder leather.
Sides may be 25 square feet or more.

moisture of the skin and form a brine which will penetrate through the hide layers. As a result of the curing, the hide will lose a lot of moisture. If it is on a slant, the brine can drain away. Never let the brine sit in puddles on the hide.

Another method is to fold the hide flesh side in after salting and then roll it up, placing it on a sloping surface to allow for drainage.

An ideal curing room has a temperature of between 50° and 55° F., humidity between 85 and 90 percent, and good ventilation but no drafts. Under these conditions, the hide will not dry out too fast before the curing is complete.

If several hides are to be cured at the same time, salt them, one at a time, then pile them on top of each other, always flesh side up, on a slanting surface. Be very careful not to disrupt the pile too much when adding new skins. Leave the hides in the pile for up to thirty days, inspecting the pile daily for heat buildup in the center, which indicates that decay is starting. If you find the pile heating up, transfer the hides one by one to new piles, adding salt before each is put in place.

After individual hides have cured a week or less and piled skins have been in the pack for about thirty days, they will be dry salted or salt hard. They will weigh about one-third less than the original green hide did, as a result of moisture loss. At this point, the hides can be safely bundled up and stored or shipped without fear of decay. Watch for insect or rodent damage, however.

Drying Hides

Although most hides and skins are preserved by salting, the oldest method is merely to dry the skins thoroughly, which denies decay bacteria the moisture they need to survive. Drying without salt must be controlled carefully, as decomposition can begin if the process is too slow, and fiber breaking and cracking can occur if it is too fast. Hides that are dried without salt are known as *flint hides* and weigh about one-half as much as the green hide. To be tanned, these hides must be thoroughly soaked and rewetted. This takes a great deal of time, and often the skins are not satisfactory for leather use.

The method used most often in commercial tanneries is called *brine curing.* It is faster and more effective, as the hides can have the salt penetration in twelve hours that would take thirty days or more to achieve with direct salting. With this process, the hides are immersed in a very concentrated brine solution which is agitated by pumps until the skins are thoroughly saturated with salt.

Curing is not tanning, but does protect the hide from bacterial decay. However, it is important to begin tanning within a few months even if you thoroughly salted the hide, to avoid damage by insects or rodents during storage. However, with excellent physical protection, salt-hard hides may be stored for up to a year in a cool, airy place. Some experienced tanners even suggest that a heavy hide that is properly salt-cured and allowed to lie in storage for a month or two tends to flesh and tan more easily and rapidly than one tanned immediately after skinning. One reason might be that salting firms the tissues so flesh can be removed more easily. Another reason is that excess fluids that might interfere with tanning have been drained away.

Handling Sheepskins

All animal skins are basically treated the same way, as described in this chapter, with one exception: woolskins. Sheepskins need a much longer period to cool than do other hides and skins because of the thick, insulating hair and the large quantity of grease (lanolin and other fats) contained, especially in the outer layers, under the hair. Salting must not begin until all the body heat is removed, and this process may take several hours on a concrete floor.

Another problem with sheepskins, also related to their tendency to stay warm, is they have a greater tendency to heat up and decompose after salting. This is a greater problem when the hide is to be tanned with the hair on, because usually wool will slip as the hide rots. Don't stack sheepskins after salting and you will lessen the chance of hairslip. Check the skins frequently during curing for any signs of heat buildup or decay and add fresh salt whenever necessary.

If you were careful during the skinning process to avoid cutting or nicking the hide, if you cooled the hide thoroughly to remove all the body heat, and if you properly cured the skin, you now have the raw material you need to make leather. Your salt-dried hide can be held in a safe place for several months before tanning if necessary, but your green, cooled hide should be tanned as soon as possible. Chapter 4 will give you all the recipes and directions you should need to turn your animal skin into a useful, beautiful piece of leather.

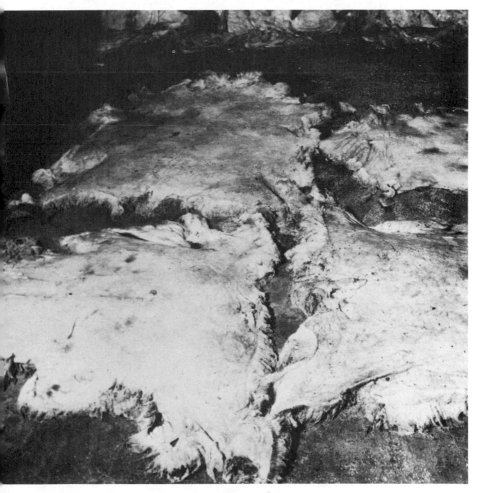

Sheepskin cooling on a concrete floor. (U.S.D.A.)

part II

Tanning

Introduction

Tanning is the process of preserving animal skins to produce leathers and furs. The history of tanning is very old—as old, in fact, as civilization itself (Genesis III, 21: "Unto Adam and also his wife did the Lord God make coats of skins and clothed them.").

The primary function of any tanning agent is to change the raw fibers of a hide, technically called collagen, into a stable product that is no longer susceptible to decay and rotting. The tanning chemicals remove the "glue" and separate and toughen the skin fibers. They also increase a hide's durability, usefulness, and beauty.

Old-timers separated the preservation processes into two groups: *tawing* referred to preserving with alum or sulphuric acid, and *tanning* referred to preserving hides with a tannic acid treatment. However, the term tanning is now used to mean any chemical treatment that changes raw hides into leather.

Most of the leathermaking today is accomplished in modern, well-equipped tanneries that employ over 32,000 people in this country alone. Some 250 tanneries scattered across the United States produce millions of square feet of leather annually. Many work in conjunction with slaughterhouses and beef producers to make the raw materials needed for the thriving leather industry which manufactures everything from shoes to handbags and suitcases. Other tanneries produce custom leathers and furs for farmers from green or green-salted hides shipped from farm to tanner. Some larger American tanneries have introduced computer-controlled equipment to speed up production and cut costs. Amateur home tanners may not be able to compete with commercial tanneries and their specialized equipment in price per skin, quality, or speed but can approach this ideal by perfecting the special skills required for successful home tanning.

Tanning Chemicals

The most important ingredient in many tanning recipes is water. For the best tanning results, use only clean, soft water with no more than a trace of minerals in it. An overabundance of dissolved minerals in the water may react with the tanning chemicals to impede the tanning process or produce undesirable hide changes. If you are using well or other water that you know contains many dissolved minerals, I suggest collecting rainwater in clean barrels to use for tanning. Rainwater is ideal to use if you can obtain enough. Use a covered collection system or strain the water through a filter to remove debris before using.

If you don't know about the mineral content of your water supply, a quick check of your toilet holding tank will give you a clue. White, green, or brown deposits on the sides of the tank mean that you have hard, mineral-rich water. Another test is to wash your hands with plenty of plain soap in a pan of cold water. If the soap curdles, your water is hard.

No matter which chemical process you are using, some basic rules must be followed. Treat all chemicals carefully and with respect. Don't mix or keep any tanning solution in a metal container. Almost all the chemicals used in this book will attack and corrode metal, and this may impede the tanning process as well. Use wood, plastic, crockery, or even rubber—but avoid metal and don't even trust stainless steel. Also stay away from using glass. Wet tanning solution containers get very slippery, and glass breaks easily. Use your tanning containers and utensils only for tanning. This way you will have them available when you need them, and you won't risk contaminating something else with tanning chemicals. Other than containers for storing and using tanning solutions, you will need glass or plastic measuring cups, a set of scales, and a wooden spoon or stick. Weigh or measure all ingredients carefully—don't guess! Mix all solutions thoroughly. Rubber gloves come in handy to protect your hands from chemicals and from contracting animal diseases. Most of the tanning recipes found in this book are not dangerous, but those containing sulphuric acid need special precautions.

Special warnings are in order when working with sulphuric acid, a dangerous chemical. Full-strength sulphuric acid can cause severe burns. Do not let it touch your skin or clothing. Do not splash it around when you are mixing, and avoid getting it in your eyes. Do not inhale the fumes. Wear safety glasses and rubber gloves for extra protection. It is especially important to avoid metal spoons and containers when working with this acid.

Skin burns can be neutralized with a baking soda paste or solution. And always neutralize the sulphuric tanning solution with a handful of baking soda before disposing of it. Watch out! It may bubble up.

Tanning Variables

Successful tanning is dependent on many variables, not the least of which is your own energy level and the time you want to spend on it. Home tanning, especially with large hides, is often a laborious, time-consuming, and messy job. I suggest that you don't begin your tanning with valuable furskins that might not come out as nicely as you'd like.

Resist the temptation to start a project that is too large, too, during your initial attempts. Stick to skins that are small to medium in size and easy to work with, such as fryer rabbits, squirrels, and muskrat.

Before you begin, you need a place to work. It should be convenient to water for washing, soaking, and solutions, damageproof (especially moisture and salt damage), and built so that splashed or spilled solutions can be cleaned up easily. I recommend a basement or garage with a concrete floor, temperature of 60° to 70° F., and away from curious animals and children. There should be space for hang-drying your tanned items and shelves to store your ingredients and equipment. Ideally, your workplace will also include a large, wooden table or a sheet of heavy plywood on two or three sawhorses for stretching out large hides as well as working with small furs. The nice part about a separate tanning room is that you keep the mess, the odor of drying skins, and the clean-up in one area instead of strewn through the entire house.

Variables

Other variables will affect your tanning efforts. First, as you learned in Part I, the condition and character of the skins and hides you choose to tan will have a great bearing on the leather that you produce. Factors such as thickness, flaws, type, and size will determine the final product.

The tanning solution or paste, its type, strength, and quantity, will also affect the condition of the leather. For instance, an oak-tanned leather will come out relatively stiff and be a dark, leathery-brown. An alum-tanned piece will be white and very supple. A chrome-tanned leather is flexible and light bluish-green.

Other factors affecting the outcome are temperature (most tanning agents work best at around room temperature, 65°–70° F.), the skills of the tanner, and the time element. Some procedures take months; others take only hours. An experienced tanner knows that if he alters the method or temperature or time at one stage of the process, quite likely it will produce an effect requiring additional adjustments in some of the following steps. When you are just beginning, follow to the letter the recipes given. Don't guess about ingredients, time, or temperature.

A couple of suggestions before you move on to the actual tanning: I do not advise reusing tanning solutions. You have no idea how potent a solution is after using it to tan one or more hides. It may not be strong enough to do a satisfactory job. If you add more chemicals to an old solution, you could make it too strong and damage the hide fibers. I recommend that you dispose of used solutions in a place away from animals (some solutions may be dangerous if taken internally), lawn, and gardens (some solutions may kill plant life). I dump mine along the paths in the woods on our property. I find that the chemical buildup in the soil keeps the pathways free of weeds. If you lack a woodlot, use a gravel driveway or similar damage-proof area of ground. One more warning—don't flush the solution into the septic tank or public sewer system, either. You may contaminate or damage them.

Some of the tanning recipes include the use of oils or fats to soften skins during or after tanning. Don't use vegetable oils on hides or skins. All greases used should be of animal origin, such as mink oil, neat's-foot oil, and similar types. Animal fats such as tallow and lard can be used, but it's a good idea to render them first to prevent off smells.

Finished rabbit furs, soft and fluffy!

chapter 3

Tanning for Fur

If you followed the instructions in Chapter 1, you should now have a supply of fur skins that is either fresh (green), frozen, or dried. Inspect the cooled, green hides carefully for flaws, areas of molt, or scarring. It is helpful at this point to slit each pelt up the belly line if it is cased (whole). If you froze your skins, defrost them in the refrigerator or by placing the unopened plastic container in cold water. If you dried the pelts, soak them in cool water until they are thoroughly wet and pliable. This usually takes several hours.

Fur tanning methods fix the hair into the pelt. *Leather* tanning processes remove the hair. That is the main difference between the two tanning methods. Because most fur skin work can be done in the kitchen sink, if no specialized area is available, starting with a small size is best for beginners.

When washing dirty pelts before tanning, use only cool water; hot water may dissolve any fat left on the skin, and it will get into the fur and make it sticky.

Pulling the flesh off a rabbitskin.

Sheepskins and certain fur skins such as opossum, beaver, and similar water animals have many water-repellent layers of fat and internal greases that cannot be removed, even in detergent. Overly fat skins inhibit tanning by repelling the tanning brine. This causes uneven tanning and leads to rotting of the finished leathers and furs. To tan these skins successfully, you need to scrape off as much fat as possible and degrease them in a solvent such as gasoline or dry-cleaning fluid prior to tanning. Sheepskins may need to be degreased before and after tanning.

Gasoline, by the way, is a superb cleaning agent, as it removes all the animal odor and oil remaining in the hair. Furs can be cleaned either by soaking them in the solvent for about an hour or by rubbing them with a saturated cloth. All degreasing operations should be done in the open air, if possible, and away from any heat source. Fumes from these solvents are as dangerous as the chemicals themselves in closed places.

Domestic rabbit is probably the most available fur skin for the home tanner. As you remember from Chapter 1, most domestic rabbits are raised for meat production, and their skins are a by-product. The medium and large breeds are best suited for both meat and fur production. The finest fur pelts come from healthy animals in prime condition. Tanning cannot improve the condition of shedding, blotchy, thin skins. Therefore, if you start with healthy, prime animals and tan the skins properly, you should be very happy with the beautiful finished furs.

Some tanning steps are the same regardless of the tanning method or solution used. For convenience, then, I will cover these common steps first before going on to individual tanning recipes.

Fleshing

Fleshing is removing the layer of fatty tissue and flesh to expose the leather (derma) to chemical actions. Even expert tanners disagree about the proper time or method for fleshing. Some say to wait until a green hide is partially dried; others say it is easier to do when the pelt is fresh; and still others recommend soaking the hide in salt water or tanning solution for two or three days. I soak my pelts for at least forty-eight hours before fleshing and I generally use an alum-salt tanning solution (see the recipes later in this chapter). After soaking, the undertissue is clearly defined and I can peel off the flesh in one piece if I am careful.

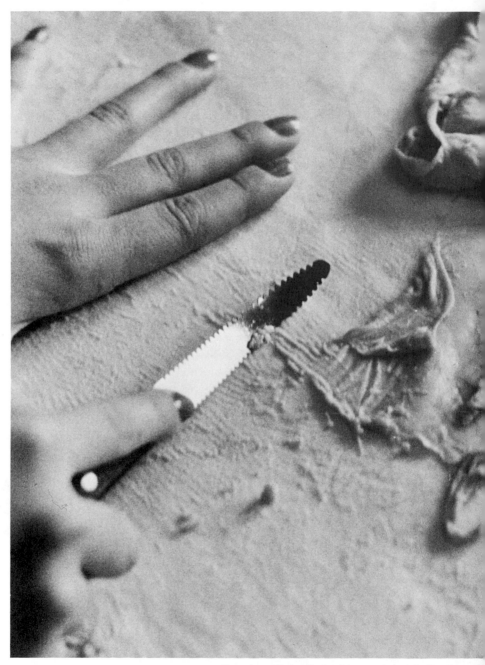

Scraping off the flesh with a grapefruit knife.

To flesh a small furskin, lay it out flat with the fur side down. Start at the tail area and work along the bottom edge first and then up both sides (the belly), staying at the edges until you reach the neck area. Use your thumbs and fingers to get under and loosen the membrane that separates the underskin from the leather layer. When the tail and belly edges are loose, take the skin in one hand and the fur part in the other and pull the skin carefully, slowly, and evenly up toward the neck and finally off the hide entirely. Flesh adhering around the neck may need to be scraped off with a dull knife.

Working from the neck down is not recommended. It is difficult to loosen the skin at the neck region and the pelt may tear more easily working downward.

Most fur-bearing animals, such as rabbits, male as well as female, have nipples on their bellies and there will be fatty places on the flesh side over each nipple. If you pull this fat off when fleshing, the nipple will come with it, and you will have a little hole in the fur. If you are careful, you can cut the fat off with a sharp knife, leaving the nipple intact.

Problem Animals

Some animals such as mature rabbits (especially males) and raccoons are not easy to flesh because the skin holds tenaciously around the legs, neck, and belly. In these cases and when working with fresh, green skins, a grapefruit knife with two-sided, serrated edges and a curved blade makes a good skin scraper.

Scraping the skin is a time-consuming, lengthy operation. It must be done with larger hides, because the flesh will not peel off as it will on a rabbit skin.

With thin furskins, it is not absolutely necessary to remove all of the fat and tissue during this step. However, the membrane that separates the underskin from the derma must at least be broken up so that the tanning chemicals can penetrate the upper skin layers. The less fat and flesh left on the pelt, the better. Don't peel or scrape too deeply and expose the hair roots or the leather will be weak. The trick with fleshing, no matter what size or type of furskin you are working with, is to do the job as slowly, to minimize tears and rips that could be avoided, and as thoroughly as you can. If the flesh won't budge from the hide, try soaking it for a couple of days or longer in a tanning solution before peeling and scraping. Be persistent and the reward will be a soft, smooth leather side of the furskin when you are finished.

Drying

After the skin has been tanned in chemicals and is still wet, squeeze out any tanning brine that is still in it. Some of the recipes include a neutralizing rinse, so follow the recipe you have chosen and don't skip steps. When you get to the part of the operation called *finishing* you will be here.

Before drying, most furskins need a final washing, usually in a sweet-smelling soap or shampoo. Adding borax and/or sassafras oil to this final wash aids in ridding furs of any unpleasant smells that might linger. After the final wash, rinse the fur several times in cool water, squeezing out the excess.

Although hand washing is most commonly employed, you can use a washing machine for this final wash. Use the delicate cycle, if you have one on your machine. Be careful not to plug your drain hoses with bits of flesh, fat, and fur from the skin.

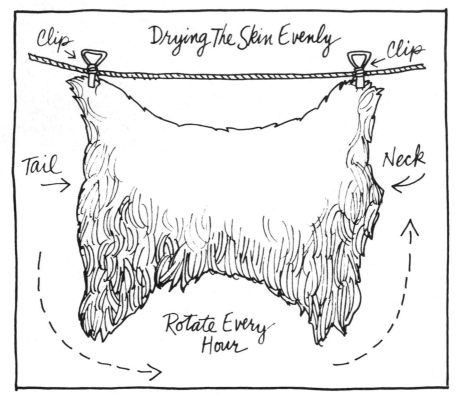

Attach the hide to a clothesline with clips and rotate about every hour or less to assure that the skin will dry evenly.

Hanging rabbit pelts to dry over a temporary clothesline in a bathroom.

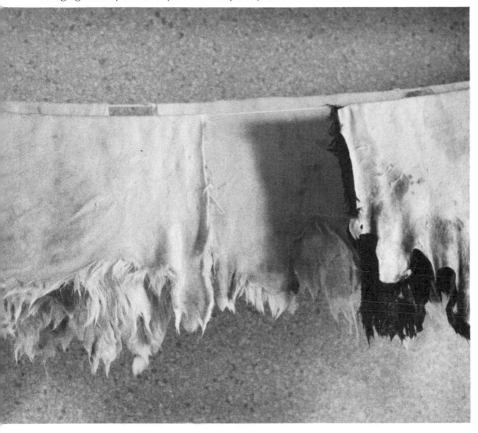

Hang the skins, flesh side up over a horizontal shaft or line, indoors or in the shade, to dry for four to seven hours or longer until only a 10–12 percent moisture content remains in the skin. This is called *equilibrium moisture*, which is the point when the skins can be most successfully softened. The skin will feel almost dry but not stiff. Drying time is dependent on a number of factors such as hide thickness, temperature, and humidity.

You will find that sections of each pelt will dry while the remainder is still very wet. To minimize this problem, turn the pelt every hour or less so that it is draped in a different position. Or you can attach the hide to a clothesline with clips and rotate the skin as shown in the illustration to assure that the hide will dry evenly. If some parts, such as the thin belly skin, still dry out faster than the rest use a wet rag or sponge to moisten these areas.

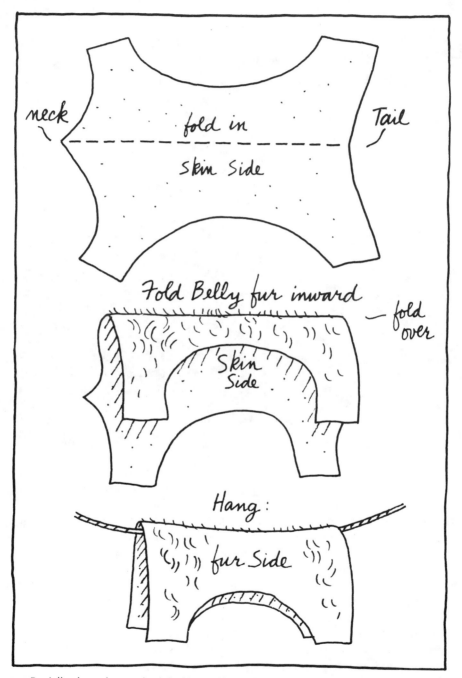

neck

fold in

Tail

Skin Side

Fold Belly fur inward

— fold over

Skin Side

Hang:

fur Side

Partially dry pelts can be left this way for a day or so without drying out too much.

Don't hang the skins to dry in sunlight or in high temperatures because they will dry out too quickly, becoming hard, brown, and worthless in no time. The trick is to maintain room temperature (60°–70° F.) and watch the pelts very carefully. When the skin is still pliable and just barely damp it has reached equilibrium moisture, the condition that you are looking for to soften and finish the tanned skins.

If you must leave the skins and are afraid they might dry out too much before you get back, fold the belly fur inward, skin to skin, and hang on a line, fur side out, as shown in the illustration. Pelts can be left this way for a day or more without drying out too much.

Commercial tanneries have several other ways to dry skins. One is called *toggling*. The wet pelt is dried in a stretched position by using clips (called toggles) along the edge of the skin which attach to a frame. The most popular commercial method is called *pasting*. The skins are pasted to a large horizontal surface with a wooden hand tool called a slicker. A starch-like material with good adhesion is added for pasting but it allows the pelts to be peeled off easily when they are at equilibrium moisture. The commercial tanners claim that they get a larger sheet of leather per hide with this method, as the pelt is held against the plate in a very stretched position until almost dry.

Breaking the Skin: Softening

This is the most important step of the entire tanning process. Even if you correctly followed all the other steps, the skin will still dry hard and stiff if you don't do this important part correctly and completely.

Since ancient times, ever since hides were first turned into leather and fur, tanners have pounded, chewed, beaten, stretched, rubbed, and worked them with or without greases and oils to make and keep the skin flexible and soft. Stretching partly dried hides to soften the leather is known as *breaking the skin*.

You cannot work a hide too much during the softening stage. The more the pelt is pulled and worked, the softer it will be.

With a small skin, like that of a rabbit, you can often work with the skin in your lap. Larger skins must be broken over a beam, sawhorse, chairback, stake in the ground, or other immovable object. (See Chapter 4 for a complete discussion of softening larger animal hides.)

Pull and stretch the skin of the damp pelt in all directions, working small areas at a time. The leather should turn soft and white. If nothing happens when you pull the skin, it has probably dried out too much or not enough. Dampen stiff, overdry skin with a sponge or by laying a wet towel over it for a few minutes until the leather is soft

Breaking the skin.

enough to pull easily. Pull slowly, but hard enough to stretch the skin to its maximum size. Pull side-to-side and top-to-bottom and all around the borders. Keep stretching for at least a couple of minutes.

Work the very edges of the pelt carefully, taking a swatch of hair and pulling away from the skin to prevent hard lines along the outer edges. After the first stretching period, hang the still-damp skin back over the line or lay it aside for a few more hours. Fold the belly skin inward if you have to leave it longer. Then repeat the breaking, stretching step. You will need a minimum of three pulling sessions before a pelt the size and thickness of rabbit is dry, supple, and soft, and more sessions for larger skins.

If you are working with several pelts and you need to leave them for a day or longer, roll all the skins together, skin to skin, fur to fur, and wrap with a damp towel or put in a plastic bag. Don't leave them this way for more than a couple of days, as the skins might mildew or spoil.

If the skin dries hard and stiff in spots, moisten the stiff areas with a cloth or sponge and repeat the stretching steps.

One of the biggest hazards of softening fragile furskins is the risk of tearing. Often a small rip will become larger and larger as the skin is stretched. Mend little tears in the leather immediately with thread and needle from the flesh side. (See Chapter 8 for more information about sewing furskins.)

Hides that have been stretched at least three times can be tacked or laced to a board or frame to dry flat, in the normal shape of the skin. This step is often recommended if you wish to cut patterns from the furskin.

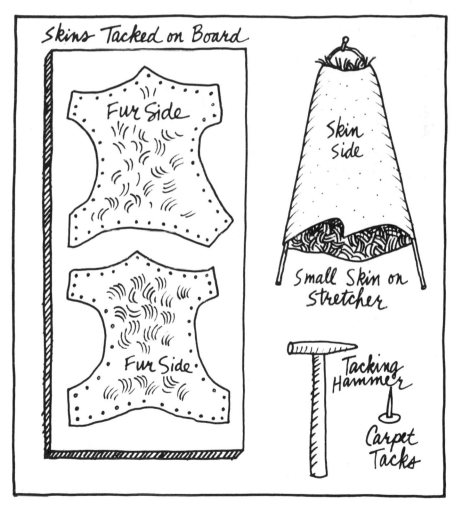

Skins Tacked on Board

Fur Side

Fur Side

Skin Side

Small Skin on Stretcher

Tacking Hammer

Carpet Tacks

Drumming

Most commercial tanneries that process furskins have large, motor-driven drums partially filled with hardwood sawdust to tumble the pelts during the drying process. This procedure softens the skin in a way similar to stretching. It also cleans and brightens the fur, removing any excess oil or grease left after tanning. The process usually takes several hours and two or three changes of wood chips. After drumming, the furskins are revolved in a wire mesh drum to remove any clinging sawdust.

You can approximate this procedure at home using a clothes dryer and skins that contain only equilibrium moisture. Tumbling the pelts in a dryer without heat for several minutes to an hour or more fluffs the fur and makes breaking the skin and softening the leather much easier.

One word of caution about using your dryer to fluff and soften furskins: Don't get in a hurry and turn on the heat. Tumbling in heated air brings oils to the skin surface and rapidly shrinks the skin. You end up with a spongy, stiff mess that won't soften, tears easily, and is very greasy. Take my advice and be patient—use only unheated dryers for this step.

If you have access to an old dryer that still spins, but has lost its heating abilities, so much the better. Convert it into a hardwood drum unit by lining the inside with aluminum foil or some other convenient material and adding a few handfuls of hardwood sawdust. Use about a pound of wood chips for each dry pound of fur. Don't use pine sawdust to clean or condition furs. It has too many resins and could tend to make the furs sticky. Maple, beech, and poplar are good hardwoods to try.

You can also use sawdust rubbed directly into the fur as a cleaning agent, either shaking or vacuuming the material out afterwards. However, most home-tanned furs don't need the sawdust treatment and a few minutes tumbling in an unheated dryer should fluff them up satisfactorily.

Other Finishing Steps

Sticky, greasy areas rarely remain in the fur after all the tanning steps are completed. However, common baking powder is an excellent grease-cutting agent to use if there are such areas. Rub a small amount of powder into the greasy section and leave it for an hour or two, then brush or vacuum it out. If the fat deposit is really heavy or deep, repeat the process.

Cornmeal is often used like sawdust to clean furs after they are tanned and dry. Many commercial fur cleaners use cornmeal. Either rub it directly into the fur or use the drumming method, then remove it by shaking, brushing, or vacuuming.

Many tanners recommend oiling the leather of a furskin as a final step to soften the skin and protect it from decay, moisture, and wear. Any oil or grease used on the leather should be worked in well, using just enough to soften but not enough to make the pelt greasy. Warming the oil before application will insure deeper penetration. Mink oil, neat's-foot oil, or even rendered animal fat can be used as leather softeners. In commercial tanneries, mixtures of oils and greases are forced into the leather by machine. This is called *tramping*.

Finals Steps

Taxidermists favor a final step that many home tanners omit. They fluff the finished furskin in a bowl or bucket of powdered borax, the same kind you buy for laundry. The borax acts as a preservative, to *poison* the skin, thus insuring complete long-term protection against rot and insect damage.

Somewhere near the end of the finishing process, you will probably want to brush out the fur. This is the fun part, anyway. A professional furrier's brush or any "doggy" type with stiff wire bristles works best. However, any small hairbrush can be used. Brush the fur in all different directions. This aids in fluffing as well as locating areas of damage, shedding, or rips. If a lot of hair comes out into the brush, chances are the fur will always shed and you shouldn't plan to use it for a garment. Prime pelts should shed very little during brushing.

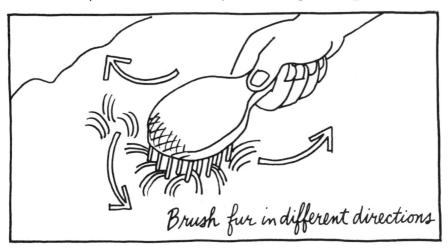

Brush fur in different directions

Finally, to give extra gloss and sheen to the fur and a light perfume to mask any remaining tanning odor, use wig conditioner spray. It comes in a can like hair spray, and can be bought in most drugstores and beauty parlors. Unlike hairsprays, it contains conditioners like lanolin. Don't use any other hairspray or spray perfume on furskins. The alcohol they contain can dry the hair, causing it to break off.

Storage

Don't store any fur or leather items, tanned hides or garments, in airtight containers. The best way to store furskins is in a cardboard box, stacked flat, fur to fur, skin to skin. If you must fold it, do it lengthwise, along the backbone only. Store the covered box in a cool place, out of the reach of rodents, insects, pets, and children.

Several species of moth larvae will strip the fur from tanned or raw skins. For the best protection, store pelts and fur garments with moth balls or naphthalene crystals, especially during the summer. A bar of sweet-smelling soap can also be put in the box with the pelts to repel insects and scent the furs.

Tanning Recipes

Alum-Salt

Alum tanning is a very popular and useful method for furskins. It will not affect the color of the fur and it acts quickly, shrinking the skin and tightening the hair follicles to better retain the fur. Alum-salt recipes are an excellent choice for furskins. They use common, inexpensive materials; the chemicals used are not dangerous; tanning can be accomplished in a reasonable amount of time; the tanning steps are easy; it doesn't take a lot of space, and usually it produces a beautifully-tanned, white-leathered pelt.

Alum has one potential fault related to its powerful astringency: it sometimes can pucker, harden, shrink, and thicken the skin and make the fur harsh and brittle—all effects which are opposite of the desired ones. Nonetheless, an alum solution can save the fur when it's starting to slip.

Alum dissolves in water. Further, it can be removed by soaking tanned skin, which could decay if left wet. Hence, alum-tanned furs and leathers should only be dry-cleaned.

Tanning with alum is more properly referred to as *dressing*. Although the alum may cause undesirable hide changes and could be leachable from the skin if the hide is kept wet for an extended period after tanning, it is still a widely-used chemical because it makes a soft, white, stretchy leather.

Potash alum, the most common alum form, is a double salt. The tanning substance in it is aluminum sulphate. In fact, when potash alum is dissolved in water, it is converted to basic aluminum sulphate. Hence, many fur dressers and tanners prefer to work directly with aluminum sulphate crystals, which are also called alum. To confuse the alum situation even more, another type, ammonium alum, is also occasionally used for tanning. All alum forms should work equally well when used in these recipes.

Common salt (fine or coarse, NOT iodized) is used with any alum when tanning skins to repress or prevent swelling of the skin fibers and to allow them to dry out soft and stretchy. The same effect is achieved when common washing soda is added to the alum for tanning.

Alum can be used as a solution or as a paste. The paste method, while more work, is preferred by most tanners for utility furs, those that are heavily used such as gloves, rugs, and coats.

Immersion Methods

Basic Alum-Salt Recipe

> 2 gallons water at room temperature (60°–70° F.)
> 2 cups (or more) salt. You can't use too much salt,
>   so use as much as will dissolve in the water.
> (2 gallons sea water can replace the above two ingredients)
> 2 cups alum, any type, powdered or granular

Mix the ingredients together in a 3–5-gallon container. This recipe will make enough solution to tan approximately six furskins the size of young rabbit hides. If you are working with larger furs or many skins, double or triple this recipe and the size of the container.

Any grades of salt and alum may be used, but the finer the grade the more quickly and easily it will dissolve. Under no circumstances should you put the furskins into the solution before all of the chemicals are dissolved. Frequent stirring will hasten dissolving.

Measure your ingredients carefully in this and all the other recipes. If the solution is too weak, the skins may rot or develop hairslip.

Salt-dried pelts do not tan well with the alum-salt method, even if they are thoroughly rewetted. If you plan to store skins before tanning with this method, it would be wiser to freeze them.

Add the skins one at a time to the solution, stirring after each addition. Leave the furskins in this solution at room temperature (60°–70° F.) for at least a week. Cooled, fresh skins can be put directly into the solution, fleshed two or three days later, then put back into the solution to finish tanning. Stirring and moving the hides in the tanning solution—at least once a day—reduces the tanning time needed as well as the risk of hairslip developing. Frequent stirring also guarantees that all areas of the hide will be tanned.

Some tanners claim that skins can be left in this solution for many months without damage as long as you stir the solution occasionally and the temperature isn't too high.

Remove a pelt that has been in the solution for at least seven days, and test it for doneness (see "Tanning Tests" at the end of this chapter). When tanning is apparently complete, remove all the pelts from the solution, squeezing the excess brine into the soaking bucket. Go on to the finishing steps as indicated in the beginning of this chapter. Some tanners recommend a quick rinse in borax-water after removing the alum-tanned furskins from the solution, but I've never used it. Borax-water is prepared by dissolving one cup of borax in a gallon of water.

Alum-Salt-Soda Recipe

> 5 gallons water, room temperature (60°–70° F.)
> 1 pound salt, or as much as will dissolve in the water
> (5 gallons of sea water can replace the above two ingredients)
> 2 pounds alum, any kind, any grade
> ½ pound common washing soda

Use a 7–10-gallon container to mix the ingredients. This recipe makes enough solution for twelve rabbitskins or a small sheepskin. Adjust the recipe for more or larger hides.

Follow the same mixing instructions for the basic alum-salt solution. This recipe is a favorite of taxidermists because it gives good stretch, flexibility, and durability.

Flesh the skins before soaking for two to five days. When a skin tests done, rinse all pelts in borax-water and then cool water.

If you want to finish your furskins by this method the way the taxidermists do, after rinsing apply a thin soap paste, made with pure soap flakes and water, to the flesh side, and allow it to be absorbed. Follow this with a thin coat of neat's-foot oil. Then go on to the finishing steps outlined at the start of this chapter. Clean the finished pelts in gasoline and warm sawdust.

Pasting Methods

Many fine furs that may become badly matted in a soaking liquid are tanned with a paste. To prepare a hide for pasting, remove the flesh and fat as soon as the fresh hide has cooled. Tack the skin, fur side down, to a smooth horizontal surface with small pins or nails around the edges.

Pasting Recipe

Mix together the following:
  1 pound alum, any kind, powdered grade
  1 gallon water
In another container, mix together these ingredients:
  4 ounces common washing soda
  ½ pound salt, fine grade preferred
  ½ gallon water

Add the soda mixture to the alum mixture, very slowly, stirring constantly. Use flour or bran to make the solution into a thin paste as thick as cream.

Any solution recipe given in this book can be used for a pasting recipe if flour or bran is added to make the thin paste.

Apply the paste only to the flesh side of the pelt, at least ⅛ inch thick. The next day, scrape off all the paste and discard it. Apply another coat, at least ⅛ inch thick. Continue scraping and reapplying at daily intervals until all the paste is used up or the hide tests done.

Paste-tanned skins can be finished as usual, but most tanners prefer to omit any washing step that requires the skin to be soaked in liquid. The skin and fur, in this case, are usually cleaned with sawdust drumming.

Acid-Salt Methods

Sulphuric acid is a popular ingredient for tanning furskins. Old-timers refer to this method as *tawing*. Acid processes are well-adapted to lightweight skins and furs because they are fast. Non-prime furskins may start to slip in a slow-acting tanning solution.

Full-strength sulphuric acid is a very dangerous chemical. Work with it carefully, respectfully, and in an area where it won't cause damage. Use only crockery, plastic, or wood containers and utensils. (See the additional warnings in the Introduction to Part II).

Basic Acid-Salt Recipe

> 2 gallons water at room temperature (60°–70° F.)
> At least 2 pounds salt (add salt until no more will dissolve)
> (2 gallons sea water can replace the above two ingredients)
> 2 ounces full-strength sulphuric acid or 8 ounces dilute
>   sulphuric acid, also known as "battery acid" or
>   electrolyte

Using a 3–5-gallon container, dissolve the salt in the water. Then drizzle the acid down the side of the container, a little at a time, stirring constantly. This recipe should tan six small skins the size of a rabbit.

Although the solution will be too dilute to harm your skin when it is all mixed together, if you stick your hand in it, you will feel a tingling sensation. Therefore, wear rubber gloves if working in acid solutions.

Depending on the thickness of the skin, a pelt can be tanned in this solution at room temperature in as short a time as three days. However, most take about as long as those done in alum solutions, or approximately a week. Again, like alum, you can flesh the pelt before tanning or after it has soaked in the solution for a couple of days. Then return the pelt to the brine to finish tanning. Stir the skins at least once a day to prevent any untanned wrinkles and to encourage faster, even tanning of the skin.

After tanning in an acid solution, the hides must be neutralized in a baking soda solution or the acid will continue to work on the skin fibers until they break. Soak and work the tanned hides for several minutes in baking soda (use a cup of soda to a gallon of water), then rinse again in borax-water for several minutes before proceding with the finishing steps.

Another way to neutralize the skins is by soaking for a couple of hours in a pail of water containing 1½ cups washing soda.

I have successfully skipped the neutralizing rinses when tanning rabbit skins. However, if you are working with furskins more valuable than rabbit, I suggest that you take the word of many experienced tanners who suggest using neutralizing rinses.

A sulphuric acid solution can be turned into a paste by the addition of flour or bran and applied to the flesh only, using the directions given with alum paste.

Skins tanned with sulphuric acid have a tendency to become damp and clammy in wet weather, as the acid-tanned fibers attract water. Further, if repeatedly wetted in this manner, many lose their tanned effect and will begin to rot. Therefore, during damp weather, store your tanned furs or fur garments in a dry area and away from any excess humidity. Also, acid-tanned skins should only be dry-cleaned.

Tanning Tests

1. Heavy Hides: Cut a thick piece of hide, preferably neck skin, and see if it is uniformly colored throughout without a darker or lighter area in the center of the skin. If the color is uniform, the hide is finished.

2. Light Skins: Pinch a fold in the skin. If a white line produced by the pinch remains when the fold is flattened out, the skins are done.

3. All Hides: The rate at which tanning is completed can be followed by determining the *shrinkage temperature* (the temperature of water at which a hide will shrink and shrivel) of the hides. As more tanning material is absorbed by the skin, the heat resistance is increased. Fully tanned leather will not change in boiling water. Untanned leather will shrivel up or become hard and rubbery. You can test a skin for doneness by putting a small piece in a pan of boiling water. If the piece does not change substantially after a minute or two, assume the entire hide is finished.

Final Thoughts

Many tanners have discovered that it seems to take less time to do one large batch of furskins than several small ones—until the finishing steps. I like to keep my tanning batches at six to twelve skins per batch, which is a convenient number for me. As a beginner, limit yourself to three to six skins per batch. Then you will not be overwhelmed when you are just learning the methods. If you have more skins than you want to work with at one time, store the excess in plastic freezer containers or bags in the freezer. Be sure to thaw them thoroughly before tanning.

Keep in mind that not all skins tan the same—even skins of the same type animal. A young rabbitskin may finish tanning in a couple of days; a mature rabbit skin may require a much longer soaking period or a more concentrated solution as well as more effort to flesh and soften. Similarly a young lambskin is a relatively easy project; a mature sheepskin more difficult and time-consuming.

Be flexible and use your common sense. Start with easy projects and when you are more skilled, move on to the harder ones. The next chapter will cover the larger animal hides that are converted to leather. If only because of the size of these hides, the methods and processes are much more difficult and time-consuming. However, the end results can be very pleasing, useful, and worth all the extra effort.

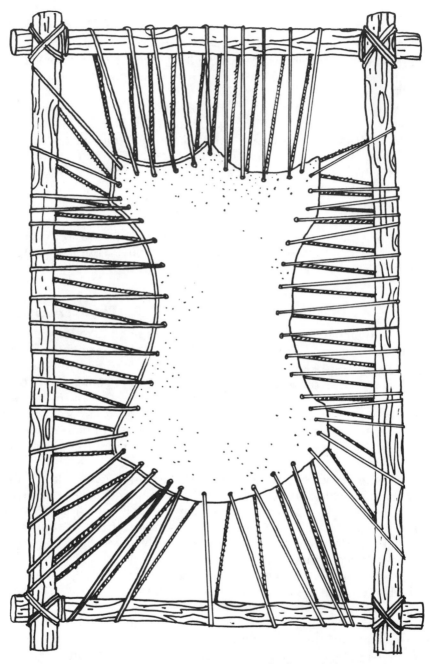

Lacing rawhide to a pole frame.

chapter 4

Tanning
for
Leather

Tanning a large, thick, awkward hide for leather production is a process that can be summed up in one word: Work! The two ingredients you will need in large quantities are elbow grease and common sense. It would be nice if some magic formula existed that immediately and forever preserved and softened hides without a lot of labor, but, unfortunately, this is not the case, especially for the home tanner.

Most of the leather we use today is prepared in large commercial establishments. Here machines do the work of several people which makes the leather tanning process faster, easier, and cheaper. Animal hides are fleshed, dehaired, tanned, rinsed, split, colored, softened, and finished, all by machine. The home tanner doesn't have these labor-saving appliances at his disposal and must rely on the simple tools of his forefathers: hand tools and a good right arm!

Nonetheless, good-quality leathers can be produced by hand at home, and the tanner will have an extra product not often available in the commercial tannery: a glowing sense of pride and accomplishment.

Tanning leathers is basically the same as tanning furs (Chapter 3) except that usually you will be working with a larger, thicker hide and the hair must be removed before the tanning step.

Fleshing

If you followed the directions in Chapter 2, you have a cooled or salt-dried skin ready for tanning. Failure to prepare the hide properly is probably the major factor leading to disappointments in leather tanning. All the flesh and fat must be removed from thick hides, and the skin of heavier ones should be shaved down.

Large, heavy hides are not simply peeled off the flesh, fat, and undertissue as can often be done with furskins. Instead, the flesh is cut or scraped off with the aid of a fleshing or hide beam. This is sometimes easier with a salted, partially dry hide. A *fleshing beam* is a piece of heavy timber or a small log, about seven to eight feet long, ten inches wide, rounded and smooth on the upper side. It is supported on one end by waist-high legs to bring the beam to chest or waist height. The peg-type legs can be set into the beam with auger holes.

Waist or Chest High

Fleshing or hide beam.

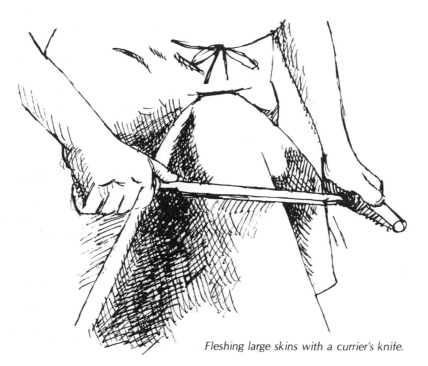

Fleshing large skins with a currier's knife.

The tanner presses against the end of the beam to hold the hide firmly between it and his body as he pushes a fleshing tool or knife away from himself, scraping or shaving off the tissue. Wood, bone, and dull knives are used for fleshing as they are less likely to damage the skin. After the undertissue is removed, a tool called a skiving knife is used to thin the leather to a uniform thickness for even tanning.

Another tool, called a *currier's knife*, has two very sharp, replaceable blades with turned edges. It is ideal for fleshing and shaving down heavy hides. However, it takes some practice, because the sharp blades can easily nick and damage the leather.

The fleshing operation resembles shaving wood with a plane. With very thick hides, it is often necessary to shave the skin all over to get a leather product that is flexible enough to be used for crafts. The thinner the skin, the softer leather it will make. However, belt, harness, and shoe leather are often left thick for strength.

Before fleshing, if the hide has been salted and dried, soak the skin to loosen the flesh enough to remove it. Fleshing is easier if the hide is salted and only dried about halfway. The salting seems to set up the flesh tissue so that it can be removed faster, and partial drying makes the skin easier to shave down in thickness.

After fleshing, soak the skins in clean, cool water before removing the hair and tanning. Washing the hides has two purposes: first, to restore the fibers to their natural shape and condition so that they will absorb the tanning agents better, and second, to remove excess salt from the tissue which could interfere with the dehairing chemicals. Partially dry hides may take from one to several days of soaking time. A handful of powdered borax in the soak water may cut this time considerably. The hide is finished when the skin is soft and the entire hide is pliable.

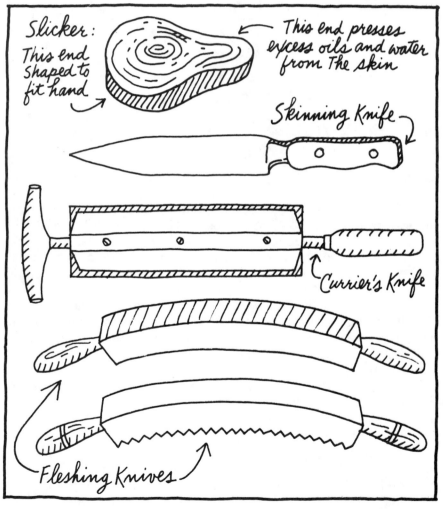

Tanning tools.

Removing the Hair

Before a hide can be made into soft, smooth leather, the hair must be removed. Some hides, like deer and elk, can be soaked in plain water for several hours. The hair will slip and be easy to scrape away. However, most skins need a depilatory agent to destroy the hair roots, loosen the epidermis (the hard outer skin surface, sometimes called *grain*, that holds the hair), and allow for their removal. Hardwood ashes, lime, and lye are common hair removal agents. Their concentration, the water temperature, and the amount of mixing of the hide in the solution all have a bearing on how fast the hair can be removed.

Dehairing solutions using lye are dangerous to work with, so wear gloves and use extreme caution. Mixing the solutions outdoors would be a good idea, too. Most depilatory solutions are not extremely dangerous, however, and those using ashes or plain water are the safest to use.

The following four separate recipes should each be enough for two medium or one large hide.

Recipe 1. 2 gallons hardwood ashes
2 gallons slaked lime
10 gallons warm water
Mix all the ingredients well. Soak the hide for three to five days, stirring occasionally, until the hair and epidermis loosen and can be scraped away.

Recipe 2. ¼ cup lye (wear gloves!)
20 gallons warm water
Mix. Soak the hide for two days in a covered container. Stir frequently. Remove when hair is loosened.

Recipe 3. 2½ pounds slaked, caustic lime
10 gallons warm water
Mix well. Soak the hide for thirty-six to forty-eight hours until hair loosens, stirring two or three times.

Recipe 4. 3 gallons hardwood ashes
10 gallons warm water
Mix ingredients. Soak the hide for three to seven days, stirring occasionally, until the hair and epidermis are loosened.

When the hair slips easily on the hide, remove it from the solution and allow it to drain for a few minutes by hanging from a clothesline, sawhorse, or tree limb. The lime water and skin scrapings have some fertilizing value, especially with acid soils. Otherwise, discard the depilatory solution.

Put the hide on the fleshing beam, hair side up, and scrape or shave off the hair and underlying epidermis in the same manner that you scraped the flesh. Work in the direction that the hair grows (neck to rump) and not against it to lessen the chances of nicks and cuts to the leather. In some cases, you can almost pull the hair off with your fingers.

Any hide that has soaked in lime or lye solutions needs to be neutralized before tanning, as the lime could interfere or deactivate the tanning agent if not removed. This process is known as a *bate* or *drench*.

Deliming

After all the hair has been removed from the skin, scrub the hide well with a stiff brush and clean water. Change the water several times.

Soak the hide in one of the following two bate solutions for at least twenty-four to thirty-six hours to neutralize any alkaline chemicals remaining in the skin. A bate soaking solution is not necessary when you use only plain water to loosen the hair. After dehairing, in this case, simply rinse the skin well in clear water and hang to drain.

Bate Solution Recipes

Recipe 1. 1 part sharp cider vinegar (weak acetic acid)
　　　　　 3 parts water

Mix enough to cover the hide. Stir well. Stir the skin frequently in the solution.

Recipe 2. 1 quart bran
　　　　　 1 gallon boiling water

Mix enough to cover the hide. Let the solution cool to about 70° F. before adding the skin. Soak at least thirty-six hours, stirring occasionally. The bran will ferment, forming an acid bate.

After the hide has soaked in the bate, remove it and let it drain until it stops dripping. Then lay the skin out flat on a piece of plywood or

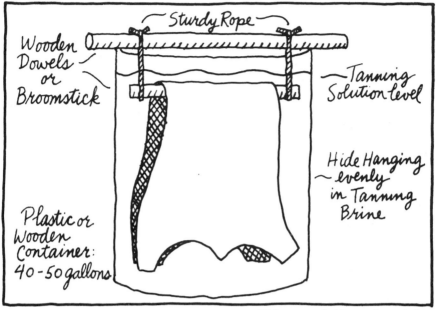

Hide suspended in tanning solution.

the fleshing beam and press out as much moisture as you can with a wooden wedge (also called a *slicker*, this hardwood tool has a six-inch blade and is shaped to fit the hand).

This operation is called *scudding*. You begin in the middle of the hide with the slicker and push the blade toward the edges. This forces the moisture out of the skin as well as flattening and smoothing the skin surface. Scud as much of the bate liquid out of the skin as you can. At this point, the skin is ready for tanning or making into rawhide.

Rawhide

Rawhide is just what the name implies: hide that is raw or untanned. It is stronger than tanned leather and can be made from just about any animal skin. Rawhide is excellent for lacing and thongs.

After you have removed the flesh and hair from your hide, punch holes along the outside edges at about two-inch intervals. Use strong rope or lacing to tie the hide to a pole frame while it is still wet. Pull the lacing tight; the tighter it is, the better the rawhide. Stretch the skin to its maximum possible size. Don't stretch so far that you tear holes in the edges, but make sure it is taut.

Dry the hide out of the sun or heat.

To use the rawhide for saddlebags, gun cases, or doggie chew toys, soak the hide in water until it is soft enough to cut with a sharp knife. Mold or lace the damp hide into any desirable form and it will dry that way.

To cut laces, after the hide is thoroughly dry, paint the flesh side with a mixture of warmed "dubbin" (one part tallow or lard to one part neat's-foot oil, castor oil, or fish oil). Warmed grease will penetrate and be absorbed better by the hide. Also, warming the dubbin mixes the solid grease and liquid oil more completely. Use a thick coat of dubbin on the rawhide, and give it an hour or more to sink in. Then pull the skin back and forth over the edge of a table or a board until it is softened enough to use for lacing. You may need to regrease or even dampen the hide several times, breaking it over the board after each oiling, before it is flexible enough to be cut into laces and used.

Tanning

Most leather tanning is accomplished in a tanning solution. For this operation, you will need a forty- to fifty-gallon container made of wood or plastic—not metal. The larger the hide, the bigger container you should use. You need room to stir the skin while it is soaking to insure that it tans evenly.

In the olden days, pioneers used a *tan trough*, which was basically a large section of tree trunk laid horizontally and hollowed out with fire and hand tools. Today a wooden or plastic pickle barrel or whiskey keg would serve the purpose well. When using wood for your tanning container, put nothing but tanning solutions in it. Wood will absorb some of the solutions it holds, so don't use it for any other purpose.

Leather can be tanned using the formulas given in Chapter 3 for furskins, but the amount will have to be increased for the larger skin. It is better to have too much solution than too little. Allow a minimum of ten gallons per medium hide and twenty gallons or more for a large one. Also adjust the time factor, as thicker hides require a much longer soaking than smaller furskins. Although salt-alum and salt-acid tanning recipes are best suited for use with furskins because they tighten the pores and retain the hair, when used with leather tanning they will produce a light-colored, almost white, leather that is stretchy and pliable.

The best use of the alum-salt recipe for leathers is as a pretan. A skin tanned in alum and salt is tanned again with a tanning method exclusively designed for leathers such as chrome, next in this chapter, or vegetable tannins as discussed in Chapter 5. The pretanning helps the penetration and fixation of the secondary tan.

Chrome Tan

Tanning skins with chromium salts was discovered near the middle of the nineteenth century. This discovery influenced the commercial tanning industry because it is a relatively rapid process when compared with older methods using vegetable tannins extracted from oak barks and other vegetation. (See Chapter 5 for a complete discussion of vegetable-oak tanning.) Today, chrome tanning is the number one method used by commercial tanneries. It produces a soft, supple leather that resists water and won't stretch out of shape.

Lightweight cattle hides, calfskin, and sheep, lamb, or goat skins are best suited for chrome tanning, but this method can be used for heavier leathers as well.

Chrome tanning agents are not soluble under alkaline conditions, and the chemical will precipitate out of the solution or go to the bottom of the brine as a solid crystal. That is why it is important that all skins dehaired with lime (an alkaline) be put through an acid drench (the bate) before chrome tanning.

The active agent in chrome tanning is most commonly known as *chrome alum*. Other names for this dark, glossy, plum-colored crystal substance are basic chromium sulphate, chromium potassium sulphate, sodium carbonate, bichromate potash, and other more complicated chemical titles. Hides tanned with chrome will turn a bluish-green throughout the skin, called the *blue state* which makes testing for tanning doneness a relatively easy task. However, this unavoidable coloring is also why this method is not suited for furskins, especially those with light or white fur.

Many different methods of chrome tanning are available to the home tanner today. I will explain three of the most common ones.

Recipe 1: The Easiest Method

> 15 pounds of chrome crystals
> 6 pounds common non-iodized salt, any grade
> 12 gallons water

The chemicals will dissolve faster if the water is warm to hot, but cool it to about 70° F. before adding the hide. Tanning will require nine to ten days for a medium hide and about two weeks for a large one. Stirring frequently will cut the tanning time considerably and will also insure that the hide tans evenly.

Recipe 2

Mix the following stock chrome tanning solution for this recipe at least forty-eight hours before you plan to use it, and keep it covered.

Part 1. 3½ pounds washing soda crystals
6 pounds common non-iodized salt, any grade
3 gallons warm water

Part 2. 12 pounds chrome crystals
9 gallons cool water
(allow time for crystals to dissolve)

When all the chemicals are dissolved and mixed, pour Part #1 into Part #2. Take at least ten minutes for this operation. Pour very slowly and mix continuously while pouring. You will now have twelve gallons of chrome stock solution, which needs to set at least two days before using.

Mix thirty gallons of cool water and four gallons stock solution in a fifty gallon barrel. Put in the hide or hides. It is best to hang them suspended from a wooden rod or broom handle so that all parts of the hide are in contact with the solution.

Mix three or four times a day for three days or mechanically agitate the solution. Remove the hide from the solution. Add four more gallons of the stock solution. Mix well and then put the hide back in the tanning brine for another three days, mixing or agitating like before.

Again remove the hide and add the remaining four gallons of stock solution. Replace the skin for four or more days, stirring as before, until finished.

Test for doneness by slicing through the skin in a thick area like the neck. The blue color should go all the way through the skin's thickness. Check the hide all over to make sure that areas of untanned skin aren't apparent.

Wash the tanned hide in a barrel of clean, cool water, changing the water three or four times.

Neutralize in a final rinse of powdered borax and water (two pounds borax to forty gallons water). Soak at least twelve hours, stirring often.

Wash the skin once more with five or six water changes. At this point, the skin can be dyed if desired. Most tanneries dye chrome-tanned leather to cover up the bluish hue it attains.

Recipe 3

For this method, start with a fleshed, dehaired, bated hide.

        Step 1. 1 gallon water
                1 pound salt, non-iodized, any grade
                ½ pound alum, any grade
                1 ounce sulphuric acid OR ¼ cup battery acid

Make enough of this solution, using the above proportions, to cover the hide and allow room for stirring. This is really a salt-alum-acid pretan. Soak the hide in this solution for a day or two, drain, and rinse well. Drain again.

        Step 2. 1 gallon warm water
                1 ounce chrome crystals

Make enough using the above proportions, to cover the skin and allow room for stirring. Soak for two or more days until the skin is evenly colored a light blue. Rinse thoroughly and air-dry several hours.

        Step 3. 1 pound hyposulphite soda
                ¼ pound borax
                1 gallon water

Make enough of this solution to cover the hide, using the above proportions. Soak the skin for one day. Wash well in plain water, and hang the hide to dry in a cool, shady place. When it is almost dry, soak in the following:

        Step 4. ½ cake laundry soap, shaved
                ¼ cake stearic acid, shaved
                1 gallon warm water
                1 cup washing soda crystals
                ½ pint neat's-foot oil

Make enough solution, using these proportions, to cover and saturate the hide. Soak at least one day in a warm place, turning and stirring the skin frequently. Hang to drain. Work the skin thoroughly to soften. Work the grain side with a slicker until smooth and hard. Sandpaper the flesh side to smooth it and remove any uneven surface areas.

Finishing

As with furskins, leather must be softened and worked by hand or machine after tanning and partially drying to insure that it will dry soft and pliable. Also, many leathers are dyed or colored while still quite damp for more even penetration of the dyestuffs.

The finishing steps depend on the intended use of the leather as well as its thickness.

Coloring

Dyeing leather is an art in its own right and requires some skill to do correctly. Several factors, such as variability among skins and penetration depth, affect the coloring, and these factors don't usually have to be dealt with when coloring almost any other substance.

Most commercial coloring of leather is accomplished with aniline type dyestuffs which are derived, in most cases, from coal by-products. Acid dyes penetrate readily, producing bright and exciting shades. Metal dyes produce subdued pastel shades. Direct dyes color the surface of the leather in a wide range of deep shades. Basic dyes color the surface in brilliant colors. Besides the coal-derived dyes found in the leather industry, several natural dyes are commonly used by the home tanner such as oak-bark extracts (dark brown color) and inks (blacks and greys, mostly). Because coloring leather is such an involved process, it is beyond the scope of this book to tell you exactly how. I would suggest that you either follow the directions given with commercial dyes obtained through a leather dealer, or color the leather after it has been finished and cut into pattern pieces. (See Chapter 7 for a discussion of this subject.)

Thick Leathers (Sole, Harness, and Belt)

After tanning and rinsing are completed, lay the hide flat across a sheet of plywood or the fleshing beam. With the slicker, push out as much moisture as you can from the skin. Work both sides of the hide well.

Coat both sides of the hide with warm neat's-foot oil. Let this set for at least thirty minutes to penetrate. Slick the hide again to remove any excess oil and to stretch the skin out smooth and flat. This process is called *setting out* and has two purposes, to squeeze out any excess moisture and grease, and to smooth and flatten the skin. Slick from the center and press hard. Continue until the skin is smooth and dry. Work over both sides. Sprinkle with warm water if it dries too fast. The hide can now be used for stiff shoe soles.

Cutting laces.

Modify this method for harness and belting leather. After tanning, slick out the excess rinse water, especially from the grain side. Coat the grain side with warmed neat's-foot oil or fish oil and tack out smoothly stretched to dry slowly. Dampen the skin until limber; then, coat the grain side with warmed dubbin (one part tallow or lard to one part neat's-foot or fish oil). Hang to dry. Remove the surplus grease with the slicker when the hide is dry. Repeat the greasing if the skin is not flexible enough.

Another procedure for thick leathers produces lacing and thongs, although the procedure for harness and belting will often produce excellent lacing as well. Cut lacing strips with a sharp knife or a special lace-cutting machine. One hide can be cut into a continuous strip by cutting the entire hide spirally, starting from the middle. To make a softer leather strip requires that the leather be worked and softened, called *staking.* This name was given because, in many cases, the leather is actually pulled back and forth across a stake in the ground to soften it. It is a method of working the tanned hides over the edge of a hard, smooth surface like shining a shoe. It's a hard way to soften thick leathers (not like working with a small furskin), but it's the only way to make leather soft and supple. Large hides are usually softened using a clamp device and a shoulder tool that looks and is used like a crutch. Often softening is easier when the hide is stationary, and the worker is using his weight to break and pull the fibers apart. Other times, the breaking tool is stationary, and the worker pulls the hide back and forth across it. Any method that works is the correct one. There are no rules except one: The longer you work at it, the softer the leather will be.

Staking beam: for larger skins.

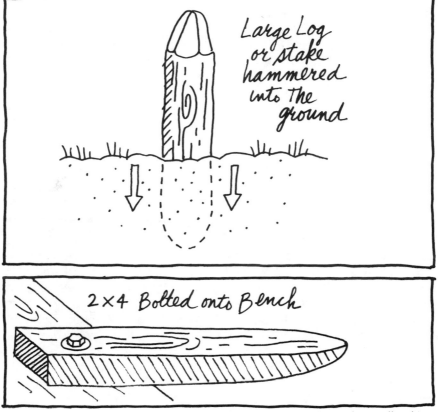

Bench beam: for smaller skins.

Follow the procedure for belt and harness leather, but before coating with oil, stake the damp hide until it is almost dry. Then, after the skin is damped and limber, before coating with dubbin, stake again. Adding these extra steps will produce a more flexible leather for lacing.

Thin Leathers (Garment)

Thin leather is both easier and harder to finish. It's easier because it is lighter, smaller, and the process more closely resembles finishing a furskin without the fur. It's harder because repeated, nearly continuous staking or softening is necessary to produce the pliability required for garment use.

Begin by letting the tanned and rinsed leather dry in a cool, shaded place. Dry it slowly and keep an eye on it so it doesn't get too dry. It should have a 10–15 percent moisture content when it has dried far enough. At that level, it will feel barely damp. At this point, it is *wet back* with a fine mist of water (a spray bottle works well) until about twice as wet (25 percent moisture). Roll the skin up and allow it to sit for a few hours or overnight to distribute the moisture evenly. Then coat the grain side of the leather with warmed neat's-foot oil. The skin should be quite limber. If it isn't, dampen further with warm water and roll up again until it is pliable. Then work it over a stake, a firm board, or any other convenient way until the leather is very soft. There is no single method for softening leather — use anything that works. Some tanners have tried such unique approaches as using a dull hatchet, a dull saw blade held in a vise, or even chewing the leather until it is soft. The thicker the leather, the longer and harder you will have to work to produce softness. If the leather still doesn't dry soft and pliable, repeat the oiling and dampening steps and stake, stake, stake again.

Commercial tanneries soften leather mechanically and use a process called *dry-milling* in which dried leather is tumbled in a large drum for one to eight hours until it is flexible. If the piece of leather you are working with is small enough, you can achieve the same effect and make staking a little easier if you tumble it for several hours in an unheated clothes dryer.

Another commercial process that you can duplicate is called *fat liquoring*. The hide fibers are well lubricated with fatty substances (dubbin works well) so that during drying, they slide readily over one another, thus regulating the leather's pliability, contributing to tensile strength, and determining how firm or soft the final leather will be.

To do this, use thick coats of oil (neat's-foot, fish, or castor), grease (tallow, lard, or solid mink oil) or a combination of the two (dubbin). Another method you might try is to use a thin, sudsy paste of good laundry soap (not detergent) applied to the flesh side after the final washing and wringing. The soap is allowed to soak in completely overnight. Then a thin coat of warm oil is applied after which the hide is dried until barely damp and staked until soft.

Other methods of tanning will be discussed in Chapter 5. However, just keep in mind that there is no easy way to do it. Nonetheless, with practice, the job will become more familiar and hence less time-consuming and labor-intensive. In the end, you should have a lovely piece of leather for craft or garment use and a glowing sense of accomplishment.

Tanning chemicals.

chapter 5

Other Tanning Methods

Vegetable Tanning

One of the oldest and most time-consuming methods of making leather from fleshed, dehaired animal skins uses the tannins extracted from oak bark and several other vegetable species. Besides being the slowest way to tan, this method also produces the finest leathers available, the only kind that can be successfully tooled or carved.

Tea leaves contain enough tannic acid to tan a very small skin or a small piece of large hide. However, the most common materials for this method are the barks of the red, white, and black oaks as well as bark from white ash, sumac, hemlock, and chestnut trees. Alfalfa and certain weeds, such as mayweed and sweetfern, also contain considerable quantities of tannic acid. In fact, nearly all woods, barks, leaves, pods, fruits, and roots contain some tannin, but most of them don't have enough to make their use for tanning worthwhile. Old trees are richer in tannin than young ones, and the lower areas of a tree have more than the top.

Oak or vegetable tanning is very laborious and takes months, in some cases, to complete. It requires about twice the hide weight in finely ground bark or other plant material or approximately 150 pounds per steer-sized hide. In the old days, tanners layered the hides in vats or pits with chopped vegetable material (usually barks) between the skin layers. Water was sometimes added but usually only the skin moisture was used to leach the tannins from the bark. The old plant material was removed and replaced every few weeks until tanning was complete. It took from six to nine months.

Today, most home and commercial tanners use an extract or infusion of the tannin-containing barks rather than the plant material itself. Barks, weeds, and other materials are gathered in the spring when the sap is up and are dried for two or three weeks in the sun or a heated room. Properly dried, bark can be kept indefinitely without a tannin content decrease. Once dried, the bark needs to be cut up in a grinding mill to the coarseness of cracked corn in order to extract the tannin properly.

Many different methods of tannin extraction and use are available, but some require high-temperature, high-pressure equipment such as is available only in commercial operations. The following two tanning methods are well-suited for the home tanner. Each recipe should be enough for a steer-sized hide or two calfskins.

Recipe 1

Pack a five-gallon container almost full with finely cut, tannin-containing materials. A variety of barks and weeds is said to produce a better tan. Cover with hot water and simmer for four to five hours. Strain the liquid from the plant material and dilute by mixing two ounces of the extract per two gallons water.

> Part 1. 8 gallons diluted bark extract (as above)
> 1 ounce salt, non-iodized, any grade
> 1 ounce alum
> ¼ ounce saltpeter
> 3 pounds terra japonica (or 1½ pounds gum gambier)

> Part 2. 40 gallons diluted bark extract
> 2 ounces salt
> 2 ounces alum

Keep the solutions separated.

Put the hide in Part #1 on the first day. Move to Part #2 on the second day and change back and forth every morning until tanned, which will take four weeks or longer. A stronger solution may tan the hide faster, but the best leather comes from a weaker solution and longer time.

The hide should feel rough. If it starts to feel slippery, strengthen the solutions: Add ½ cup terra japonica or ¼ cup gum gambier to Part #1, and two quarts of diluted bark extract to Part #2.

Test to see if the hide is tanned by slicing through the neck skin to see if the brown color goes evenly through the entire skin thickness. If it does, drain it and rinse it well in clear water. Finish as in Chapter 4, belt and harness leathers.

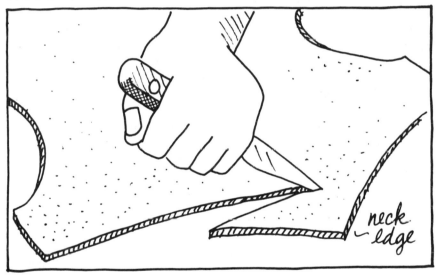

Recipe 2

Begin this infusion about two or three weeks before it is needed. Mix forty pounds of ground bark with thirty gallons of boiling water. Stir well. Keep the mixture covered and stir occasionally. When ready to use, strain through burlap. Rinse the bark with ten gallons of fresh water, strain, and add to the previously strained liquid. You should have thirty-five or forty gallons of liquid extract. Add two quarts of any vinegar and mix well. Hang the fleshed, dehaired hide in the solution. Keep the skin suspended in the solution from a wooden rod or broom handle so that all parts of the hide are in contact with the brine and hence tan at equal rates. If you don't do this, move the hide around several times a day.

Prepare a second infusion extract the same as before using another forty pounds of bark, thirty gallons of boiling water, etc.

After the hide has hung in the first solution for about two weeks, remove the skin and take out five gallons of the solution. Add five gallons of the second extract and two quarts of vinegar to the original solution and stir well. Replace the hide.

After another week, repeat this process, adding another five gallons of the second extract but no vinegar. Repeat the five-gallon replacements at weekly intervals until the second infusion extract is used up. This means five or six more changes.

Approximately thirty days after you started the tanning, mix a third infusion with forty pounds of ground bark and just enough hot water to moisten it. Keep it covered until used.

When the hide has soaked forty-five to fifty days in the solution, remove and inspect a slice in the neck for progress. You should see a brownish line coming in toward the center from each side of the hide. Mix the moistened bark from infusion #3 into the tanning solution. Put the hide back in the barrel for another three to five months, stirring it occasionally and inspecting the tanning every few weeks. Add enough water or fresh bark to keep the hides covered if needed. Leave sole leather another two months after tanning is apparently complete.

When tanning is finished, spread the hide flat and scrub both sides well with a stiff brush and plenty of cool, clean water. Using a wooden wedge or slicker, scud as much liquid from the skin as you can. Paint the flesh side with neat's-foot oil and hang the hide in the shade to dry. Dampen the skin until it is flexible, and smooth the flesh side with a fleshing knife or slicker. Soak the skin in water until very soft, and lay on a flat, smooth surface. Scour both sides with a scrub brush. Sleek in all directions, again and again, with a slicker. Apply a heavy coat of the following dubbin to the flesh side:

> 2 pounds melted tallow
> 3 quarts neat's-foot oil
> ½ cup kerosene

Warm the ingredients and mix together thoroughly before applying. Rub off any excess dubbin with burlap. Smooth the hide again with a slicker. The leather, when dry, can be used for harness, belting, or shoe leather. If the leather isn't soft or flexible enough, dampen again and add another coat of dubbin, repeating the final smoothing with a slicker. Black harness oil can be applied as a final step if the leather will be used for harnesses.

Because vegetable tanning dyes the skin a brown, leathery color, it is not recommended for furskins unless the coloring is not objectionable. However, sheepskins tanned with tannic acid can be very stunning, with brownish wool and matching leather.

The following method, called *bag tanning*, is useful for woolskins when the tanner wants a brown leather but an uncolored wool.

Sew the sheepskin, wool side out, so that it forms a bag, or use a cased (uncut) skin. Leave the neck open and use it as a funnel. Clamp or sew the bottom closed. Suspend the bag over a bucket from a pole. It will drip.

Pour any bark infusion recipe into the neck area and fill the skin. Leave it hanging until the infusion penetrates the skin. Clamp the neck closed and turn the skin over. You may need to reverse the skin from top to bottom several times to tan the skin evenly. Keep the bag full, adding fresh infusion as needed. Tanning is complete when the brown color penetrates through the skin layers. Empty the bag when finished. Wash the skin lightly and finish as with furskins in Chapter 3.

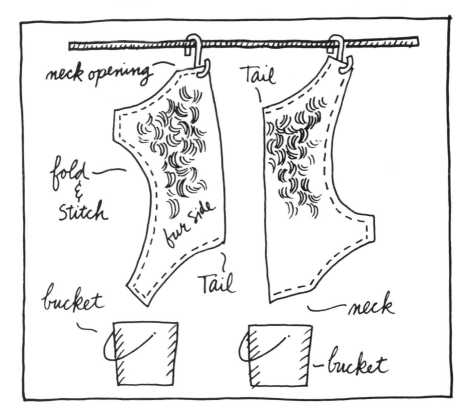

Retanning

Retanning or combination tanning combines the best properties of more than one tanning agent. In effect, it is a double tannage. For instance, a alum-salt tan can be followed with a chrome or vegetable tan or a chrome tan by vegetable tanning.

Mineral Tanning

Alum-salt, acid-salt, and chrome tanning are all examples of mineral or chemical tans used in today's most popular methods. Several other chemical recipes are used by commercial and home tanners.

Alum-Washing Soda Recipe

This solution produces a very white leather and is suitable for both furskins and leather hides.

> Part 1. 5 gallons water
> 6 pounds salt, non-iodized, any grade
> 3 pounds washing soda
>
> Part 2. 15 gallons water
> 12 pounds potash alum

Mix two solutions separately; then add Part #1 to Part #2 very slowly. Take as long as ten minutes so that the solution doesn't turn milky. Leave the skins in the combined solution a week or longer, stirring often. When tanning is complete, rinse the skins for fifteen minutes and hang to dry. Soften and finish as with furskins (Chapter 3) or garment leathers (Chapter 4).

Oxalic Acid Recipe

This formula is good for small pelts, but it is very poisonous, so handle with extreme caution. It produces an open, porous, white leather.

> 1 gallon water
> 2 cups salt, non-iodized, any grade
> 2 ounces powdered oxalic acid

Prepare two or three gallons for a sheep or calfskin. Small furskins will tan in approximately twenty-four hours, medium skins in two to three days. Stir the skins in the solution occasionally to insure even tanning. After tanning in oxalic acid, soak the skin overnight in the following neutralizing rinse:

> 5 gallons water
> ½ cup washing soda

Rinse in clear water and hang to dry until damp. Finish as for furskins, Chapter 3, stretching and working the leather to soften it.

To use the oxalic acid formula for heavier hides, add six ounces of gum catechu dissolved in a little hot water to each gallon of the oxalic acid solution above. Tanning will require one to two weeks, and the leather will be a nice tan color and waterproof. Finish as with garment leathers, Chapter 4.

Carbolic Acid Recipe

> Step 1. 1 gallon water
> 1½ tablespoons carbolic acid crystals

Using these proportions, make enough to cover the skin. Soak the hide in this solution overnight or until soft.

> Step 2. 1 gallon water
> ½ pound salt
> ¼ pound potash alum
> ½ ounce carbolic acid crystals

Use the above proportions and make enough to cover the skin. Soak the hide in this solution for about a week or until tanned. Remove the skin and hang until it stops dripping. Paint the flesh side with a coat of sulfonated neat's-foot oil and hang until barely damp.

Work over a stake or beam and finish as with garment leather, Chapter 4.

Oil Tanning

Oil-tanned leather is basically rawhide that has been saturated with various oils and greases. Three or more applications of warmed neat's-foot oil, castor oil, fish oil, or dubbin are rubbed into the skin which is then allowed to sit in a warm place until all the oils are absorbed. The leather is then staked and worked until it reaches the degree of softness desired. Oil tanning is an effective way to waterproof leather, and the oil may be applied during use for further protection.

Buckskin

An old-fashioned type of leather made from the skins of deer, elk, and caribou has been used in this country for decades. The North American Indians were adept at making buckskin for their moccasins, tepees, and garments, and they taught their techniques to the settlers.

Properly made, buckskin is as soft as chamois and stronger and warmer than cloth—plus, it is briarproof. Buckskin is really not a tanned leather, but rawhide made soft and supple with oils, smoke, and continuous working while it is drying.

Making Buckskin from Deer Hides (Yields)

Dressed deer weight	Hide size	Buckskin yield
90–130 pounds	Small	6–8 square feet
130–175 pounds	Medium	9–11 square feet
175–200 pounds	Large	12–15 square feet
Over 200 pounds	Extra large	16–18 square feet

Indian Buckskin

Soak the hide in water or water with a handful of wood ashes thrown in until the hair begins to slip. This takes one to two days. Using a fallen tree as a fleshing beam and a thighbone or rib of the butchered animal, scrape off all the flesh and fat as well as the hair and epidermis.

Mix the animal's brain and loose fat (tallow) with hot water and simmer until it forms a thin paste. Remove from heat and cool. Smooth out the lumps with your fingers. Rub this paste into the hair side of the skin with your hands and allow it to set overnight.

The next day, when the hide is partially dry, pull and stretch or scrape with bones and stones until the leather is soft and pliable.

Make a slow fire with wet, green wood (to produce a brownish color) or rotten wood (to produce a yellowish color). You want lots of smoke but little flame. Too much heat will burn the buckskin. Raise a tepee frame over the fire pit and lay the buckskin over the frame. Several skins can be smoked at once. Smoke the skin for three to five days until it turns a nice brown or yellowish-brown color all over.

The buckskin is now ready for use.

Other optional methods include: after the brain paste is rubbed in, roll the hide and let it set for a couple weeks; or smoke the skin before softening. If you smoke it first, you will have to soak it in water to regain pliability before staking.

dig pit
1' deep × 2' wide

green or well rotted wood

1'

2'

tie 4 poles together at the top

arrange hides over poles

lots of smoke and little flame

White Man's Buckskin

Dehaired calf and sheep skins make acceptable deerskin substitutes. Dehair and flesh the hide as outlined in Chapter 4. Grease the flesh side of the skin well with any animal fat or oil such as lard, tallow, neat's-foot oil, or fish oil. Hang the hide for two days in the shade.

Mix together a strong tub of soapsuds. Dissolve the soap in a little warm water first. Soak the hide in this solution for four to ten days or until the soapy water can be easily squeezed through the skin. If you store the hide and solution in a moderately warm place (about 75° F.), the time needed will be decreased.

Rinse the skin in clear water and wring it dry, removing as much water as possible. Stake and soften the skin until dry, working it more or less continuously. The secret of supple buckskin is this continuous working.

Smoke it over a slow fire or in a smokehouse for the traditional color and buckskin odor. This smoking step also prevents the buckskin from drying hard when it gets wet.

Buckskin can be given a buff color without smoking by spreading yellow ochre evenly over the skin surface when the hide is dry and rubbing it in with a stiff brush.

Sheepskin

Although woolskins can be prepared either like furskins (Chapter 3) or like dewooled leathers (Chapter 4) or even like buckskin, several special methods have been adapted specifically for sheepskins.

Alternative Sheepskin Tanning Methods

To avoid soaking the wool, paste the skin side only with any of the tanning pastes mentioned in Chapter 3.

To save the wool when dehairing, sheer the sheep close to the skin before slaughter or after the hide is removed from the carcass. Then paste the hair side of the skin with the following:

> 1 part slaked lime
> 2 parts hardwood ashes
> Enough water to make a thick paste

Roll up the hide and lay it away in a warm room for a few hours until the short wool and epidermis are loosened enough to be scraped away.

Sheepskin Mats

Wash all the dirt out of the wool with a strong soap solution and several rinses of clear water. Using the fleshing beam, remove all traces of flesh and fat. Tack the skin out in a relatively rectangular shape, wool side down, to dry. Cut off any uneven edges. When the skin is just barely damp, sprinkle the flesh side with one ounce each powdered alum and saltpeter. Let the skin finish drying. When the skin is thoroughly dry, rub the flesh side with your hands and pumice stone or sandpaper. The mats are now ready to use.

Glutaraldehyde Tanning

The U.S. Department of Agriculture has an excellent home-tanning process for sheepskins that produces woolskins that can be laundered in the washing machine. William F. Happich, inventor of this process, developed his method for making washable sheepskin bedpads for hospitals and nursing homes. It had long been accepted that woolskins prevented bedsores by evenly distributing the person's body heat and absorbing excess perspiration. But because wool bedpads required special care to launder, they were not widely used before this process became available.

Washable sheepskins can be used in many ways besides bedpads. They can be used as car and truck seat covers, throw rugs, and even coats and jackets.

To begin, wash the sheepskin thoroughly in a solution of ten gallons water, not warmer than 90° F., and one cup soap or detergent. Wash for at least five minutes. Repeat the process until the skin and wool are thoroughly clean. Scrape and peel all the fat and flesh away from the leather layer and rinse again.

Place the skin over a fleshing beam or wooden sawhorse and let drain for twenty to thirty minutes. Squeeze any remaining moisture out of the skin and wool by hand. Weigh the hide and record the weight.

For each pound of woolskin, place the following ingredients in a clean barrel. Use wood, plastic or stainless steel — no iron or galvanized metal.

> 1 gallon of 70° F. water
> ½ pound non-iodized salt, coarse or fine grade
> 2¼ fluid ounces glutaraldehyde (25 percent commercial solution)

Stir the solution well. Glutaraldehyde is an irritant. You should avoid contact with your skin or eyes and don't inhale the vapors.

Immerse the cleaned, fleshed woolskin carefully in the solution, then stir for about five minutes with a wooden paddle. Thereafter, stir for one minute every hour during the first day. Cover the barrel with a wooden lid when not stirring and overnight. The wool color will become pale yellow as the tanning proceeds. Continue stirring at hourly intervals the second day. Tanning will require at least forty-eight hours to be complete.

Test for tanning doneness by boiling a small piece of hide in water. The tanned skin should not shrink substantially. Although tanning can usually be completed in forty-eight hours, a fuller, softer leather results if the woolskin is left in the solution an additional six to eight hours.

Drain the tanned sheepskin over a sawhorse, then wash in several changes of clear water. Hang the skin, wool side up, over a fleshing beam, sawhorse, or stout rope overnight.

Apply a thin layer of neat's-foot oil or fish oil on the flesh side of the sheepskin. If the hide was particularly greasy, this step can be eliminated or you can use very little oil. Cover the hide, flesh side up, with a piece of plastic and leave overnight.

Place the skin, wool side up, over a sawhorse and dry the wool. An electric fan or a stiff outdoor breeze will speed drying. Then nail the skin, wool side down, to a piece of plywood. Stretch the skin evenly and place the nails every five to six inches. When the flesh is nearly dry, pull out the nails and soften the leather by pulling it over a ground stake, table edge, or other hard, smooth object. Repeat the pulling and

Romney: long wool breed & big bodied.

Shropshire: Black Fibers in wool

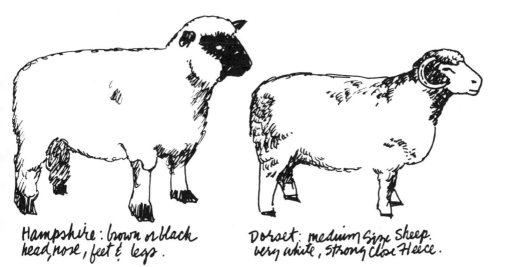

Pull and work leather until dry

working of the leather at intervals until it is dry. If it isn't soft and pliable enough, dampen the flesh side with water and cover with plastic for several hours or overnight until it can be worked again.

The flesh side can be smoothed with sandpaper or pumice to make the final leather softer and more flexible. The wool should be combed out carefully with a metal comb.

To wash sheepskins tanned by this method, use moderately warm water and a mild soap or detergent. Wash only five minutes, as longer washing could mat the wool. Rinse in cool water. Spin to extract the excess water. At room temperature, hang to dry for about forty-eight hours.

Hampshire: brown or black head, nose, feet & legs.

Dorset: medium size sheep. very white, strong close fleece.

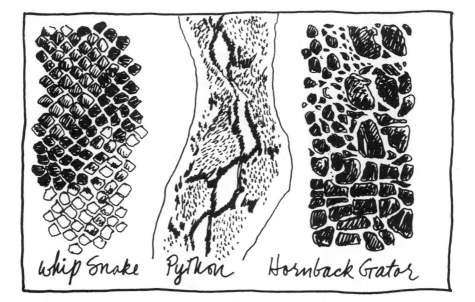

whip Snake   Python   Hornback Grator

Snakeskins and Other Novelty Leathers

Tanning Snakeskin

Snakeskins are hard to generalize about since they can vary considerably in thickness according to the length of time since the animal last shed its skin. Even a very old snake can have a thin skin if it recently went through a molt.

As soon as possible after removal, flesh as much fat and tissue from the snakeskin as you can, using a spoon. Scrape off the scales in much the same way as scaling a fish or the leather won't be flexible.

Snakeskins can be dried using a method similar to rawhide or they can be tanned using the alum-salt or acid-salt recipes given in Chapter 3. Or you can try soaking them in 70 percent (140 proof) alcohol for several days.

The following tanning method was developed specifically for snakeskins:

Step 1. Put the fleshed, descaled skin in the following solution:

        1 ounce boric acid
        1 gallon water

Soak for twenty-four hours in this solution, then rinse thoroughly in clean water.

Step 2. Soak the skin for three or four days in the following solution:

> 1 gallon water
> ¼ pound salt, non-iodized, any grade
> 15 grams chrome alum

Step 3. Remove the skin. Mix this solution:

> 5 grams sodium carbonate
> 1 cup water

Step 4. Add it to the chrome solution drop by drop, stirring constantly. Soak the snakeskin in the combined solution for a week, stirring daily. Drain.

Step 5. Soak the tanned skin overnight in the following:

> 1 part sulfonated neat's-foot oil
> 3 parts water

Step 6. Drain and wipe off the skin. Tack to a board to dry. Work and soften the skin carefully by drawing across the edge of a table. Polish by pressing the scale side with a smooth, warm iron, using a pressing cloth or heavy paper between the skin and the iron, to flatten the skin. Coat with a flexible plastic spray or rub briskly with a cloth saturated with thin shellac. The most popular use of tanned snakeskin is for hatbands.

Alligator

Soak skin in a strong lime bath (½ pound slaked, caustic lime in 2 gallons water) for a week or more, followed by bating as outlined in Chapter 4. Tan as for shoe leather.

Shark

Sharkskin is usually treated like rawhide. It is difficult to tan because the skin is almost impervious to water. It is also very difficult to soften properly. But because of these conditions, sharkskin rawhide is waterproof, strong, and virtually puncture-proof.

Hairslip in a center of molting fur. Notice the shorter fur nap in the molt area.

chapter 6

Trouble-
shooting

Tanners apparently have many common problems with their leathers and furskins. I have received the same questions over and over again from beginners, and I think it would be helpful at this point to answer these questions for you, before they come up.

Question: WHAT ARE SOME HIDE DEFECTS THAT I SHOULD LOOK FOR AND AVOID?

Answer: Several problem areas or defects in hides used for fur and leather make the end product less valuable. When possible, avoid skins marred by defects I've listed below because the time you spend tanning and finishing these skins will just about be wasted when you see the inferiority of the final product. Remember that tanning cannot improve or change the condition of the skin at the time of butchering. Basically, tanning only preserves the skin against future decay.

1. Brands. Most cows are branded on the hindquarters which is the best piece of hide, from the leathermaker's point of view. Often you can work around this defect or even use it as a decorative part of a project. Usually, however, the hide, and hence the leather, is weak at the brand point since it is, after all, a scar, and all scars weaken leather. Many wise cattle raisers aren't branding these days but are marking their cattle with ear tags, ear numbers or other inconspicuous forms of identification that prove less damaging to the hide.

2. Grub holes. The larvae of the warble fly develops in the back of cattle, just under the hide. It punctures the hide to breathe and eventually leaves the animal host through this hole. Although this parasite is little more than an irritant to the living animal, the holes and scars left by the larvae weaken the leather along the back. In fact, some of the holes never heal, and the final leather is full of holes in the thickest part of the hide, along the backbone. The best way to avoid this problem is to spray or powder all cattle with pesticide to kill the fly before the eggs can hatch into troublesome larvae.

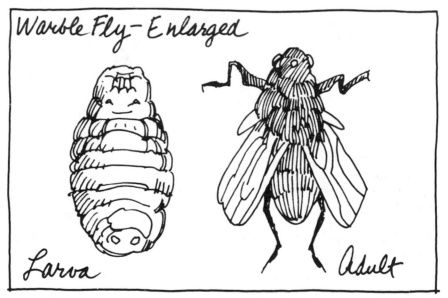

Warble Fly — Enlarged

Larva

Adult

3. Cuts, scratches, and other sores are major flaws in any leather or fur product. They tend to be worse on fur because the hair is slow to grow back in the damaged area. Many such defects are caused by accidents, such as an animal rubbing a barbed-wire fence. However, some are caused by inappropriate handling of the live animal. Caged furbearers are notorious for fighting among themselves if too many are caged together, and otherwise prime fur coats get damaged. There is nothing you can do to repair the damage caused by unhealed wounds in the skin. The best answer is not to slaughter the animal until the sore has healed. Scars are defects, too, but not as bad as unhealed wounds. Try to eliminate circumstances where the animal can so injure itself.

4. Chewed fur. Furbearers often chew on their own or their neighbor's fur if they are subjected to overcrowding or nutritional problems. Shorter nap areas or fur missing are indications that this problem exists. Don't slaughter these animals until the fur has grown back in, and do something to improve their conditions so that it doesn't happen in the future.

5. Molt. Probably the biggest cause of frustration when tanning furbearers is shedding caused by molt. Molt is a normal, natural process that every fur-bearing animal goes through. It is related to growth and seasonal changes. Chapter 1 has a discussion of molt and its causes as well as how to detect it in a living animal. A furskin tanned during a molt will continue to shed. Try to pick furskins that are prime, or mostly free of shedding, for the best results.

Question: WHAT ARE "BUTCHERING DEFECTS" IN THE SKIN— AND HOW DO I AVOID THEM?

Answer: The pre-tanning stage is very important if you want premium leather and fur after tanning.

The most common butchering defects—cuts, scores and skin slices—are caused by carelessness and doing the job too quickly. When using a skinning knife, work slowly and with care. Keep the blade turned toward the meat rather than the skin—and do as much of the removal with your fingers as you can.

Another butchering problem is poor pattern and trim. Again, this defect can be avoided by making all cuts slowly and exactly. The opening cut along the belly line especially should be very precise to assure proper pattern to the hide. Trim all ragged areas and uneven edges shortly after the skin is removed from the animal.

Question: WHAT CAUSES THE FUR TO "SLIP" OR PULL OFF THE PELT IN CLUMPS? CAN I DO ANYTHING ABOUT IT?

Answer: *Hairslip* is an indication that decay has begun in the upper, hair-containing layers of the animal's skin after its removal from the carcass. It results in bare areas in the fur and possibly a disagreeable odor during tanning. Also, the leather in the hairslip area may dry stiff and brittle, no matter how much you try to soften it.

This condition, for which there is no cure, may be caused by a variety of factors, including:

1. Molting. Fur shedding may weaken the skin and be an indirect cause of hairslip. At least molting areas seem predisposed to this condition.

2. Improper or incomplete cooling of the skin after it is removed from the carcass. Heat retained in the skin causes decay faster than any other condition. Keep in mind that a pelt's heavy fur coat tends to keep this body heat near the skin, too. So pay extra attention to proper and complete cooling of all furskins after butchering to prevent decay.

3. Crowding pelts in the tanning solution may form wrinkles in the skin that are not exposed to the tanning brine. Hairslip will develop in these untanned wrinkles. Not stirring the skins often enough during tanning may also cause this wrinkle-hairslip problem. Also, if the tanning brine is too weak, some or all of the furs will develop hairslip.

Question: WHAT HAPPENS IF I DON'T RINSE THE TANNING SOLUTION OUT OF THE SKIN BEFORE DRYING AND FINISHING?

Answer: Several things may occur. For instance, if you used an acid solution to tan your skins, the acid could continue to work on the skin fibers after the hide was removed from the brine, and eventually the skin would deteriorate as the hide fibers grew weaker and began breaking apart. Other possible outcomes might include:

1. The salty skin could draw moisture from the air on damp and humid days and could begin to feel slimy.

2. The fur could feel salty and gritty.

3. The salt could deposit in the skin and leave a "prickly" feeling in the leather. This condition can also result from adding skins to the tanning brine before all the salt has dissolved.

4. The leather could dry with white salt stains in or on it.

Question: I STORED SOME OF MY TANNED FURSKINS IN BOXES IN A SHED. THE ROOF LEAKED AND MY PELTS GOT DAMP. I DIDN'T DISCOVER THIS RIGHT AWAY AND WHEN I DID, I FOUND LITTLE PINK DOTS ALL OVER THE SKIN OF THE DAMP HIDES. WHAT IS THIS? ARE THEY RUINED?

Answer: What you found was probably a mold or fungal growth that occurred under the moist conditions. I've seen this problem, too. Try drying the pelts thoroughly, stretching and working as necessary to keep the leather soft and pliable. Once the skin is dry, the mold growth will be stopped. There is no way to remove the pink spots, however, and there is the possibility that the leather has been weakened by the growth. Don't use these skins for fur garments—but they should be safe to use for lining slippers or mittens or for small handicraft items.

Question: I THOUGHT I FOLLOWED ALL THE DIRECTIONS, BUT MY SKINS CAME OUT AS STIFF AS CARDBOARD! WHAT CAN I DO?

Answer: This problem probably arose during the softening stage of the tanning process. Evidently the leather was not stretched and worked enough during drying. Rewet the skin with a sponge or a damp towel until it is pliable, and then work, stretch, and pull the leather again until dry.

Some animals just have tough skins to soften—mature, male rabbits, for example, are particularly notorious for this problem. In fact, if breeders want to use males for fur animals when they are mature, butchering them when they are 5½ to six months of age, the young animals must be castrated between eight and twelve weeks of age to prevent thickening and toughening of the skin. Basically, any animal will have thicker, harder-to-soften skin when mature than a young animal of the same type, and males usually have tougher skin than females.

Undertanned skins often dry hard. Be sure to use one of the tanning tests in Chapter 3 to make sure the hide is completely tanned. If the skin is undertanned, the reason might be that it wasn't in the solution long enough, it wasn't fleshed thoroughly and the solution couldn't penetrate, or it was too greasy and repelled the tanning solution.

If the skin didn't soak long enough, put it back into the brine for a few more days. It doesn't hurt for a hide to soak longer than necessary.

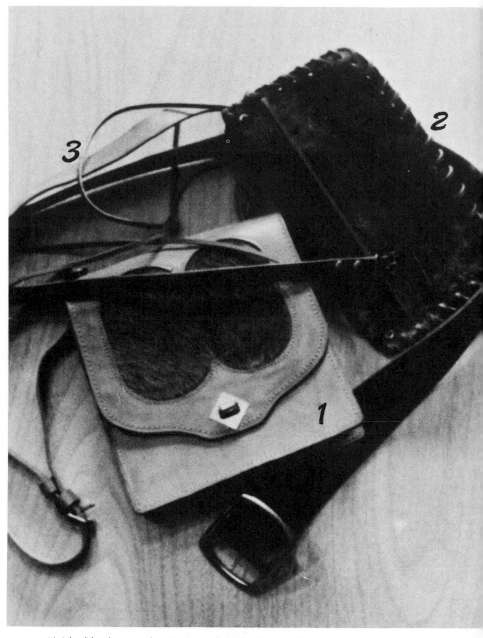

Finished leather goods: 1) *An undyed leather handbag made of oak-tanned calfskin, the insert having the hair left on.*
2) *A wallet made from dyed and finished rabbit leather.*
3) *Two belts.*

part III

Leather & Fur Crafting

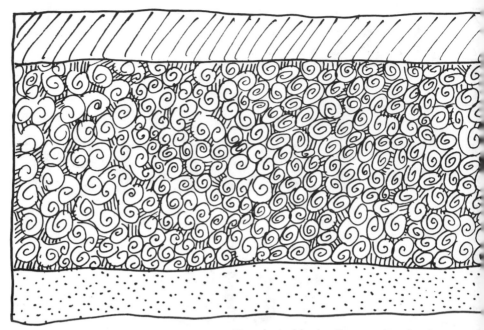

Hypothetical leather X-ray section showing the coiled corium structure.

Introduction

Sewing with leathers and furs is a craft as old as man's need and desire for clothing and footwear. The first leather craftswoman used needles of bone, thread of sinew, and scissors of flint to fashion clothing for herself and her family. In recent years, working with leathers has gained a wider popularity both as a means of creating fashionable wearing apparel and as a profitable hobby. Skin and leather items can often be designed for the price of a ready-made plastic imitation or less if you tan the hide yourself, and the hand-made factor adds an aesthetic value not available with the store-bought variety.

Leather is a valuable product of nature offering the inherent qualities of prestige, durability, eye-appeal, and unsurpassed healthful properties. All leathers are classed as flexible sheet materials which also include textiles, paper, sheet rubber, certain plastics, and like materials. Leather is actually one of the strongest flexible sheet materials known because of its corium structures. In the corium, millions of coil-like collagen molecules are built into fibrous strands that are twisted together to form bundles in a three-dimensional manner. This gives

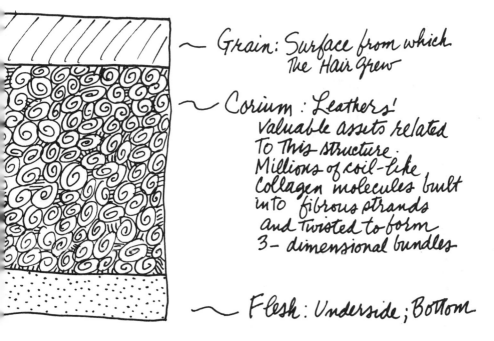

~ Grain: Surface from which The Hair grew

~ Corium : Leathers' valuable assets related To This structure. Millions of coil-like Collagen molecules built into fibrous strands and Twisted to form 3- dimensional bundles

~ Flesh: Underside; Bottom

leather a very high tensile strength. Also, because of the random distribution of the fibers, leather has an extremely high resistance to tears; it can be stretched up to 60 percent of its unstretched length without breaking, although this elongation factor is controlled somewhat by the tanning process.

Other properties of leather include its excellent flexibility over a wide range of temperature and moisture conditions and resistance to punctures, again relating to the irregular, random fiber pattern. All these factors contribute to the long life of most leather goods, such as shoes and gloves, but they can also make most leathers difficult to sew as needles cannot penetrate easily.

Leather's fine network of millions of tiny fibers linked together into the corium structure permits the leather to breathe, that is there is a steady movement of air and water vapor within the structure. For this reason, it is important that leathers be stored properly, avoiding airtight containers. Most large sheets of leather are stored by rolling the hides up with the good surface facing the inside. The rolls are stored on shelves. Smaller pieces of leather and furskins can be stored in loosely covered cardboard boxes. Finished leather and fur items can be stored in fabric (not plastic) clothing bags or boxes.

Types of Leather

The surface or grain characteristics as well as many other qualities differ among different leathers. In the industry, leathers are graded for such factors as uniformity of color, thickness, and the extent of any defects which appear on the surface. If you are working with home-tanned leathers and furs, you will not be so concerned with the grade. However, if you go to a leather store and purchase hides for garment and craft use, it will pay to be knowledgeable about what you are buying.

Cowhide: A uniform, durable, very workable leather.

Equine: (Horses, mules, donkeys) Similar to cowhide, but coarser grained and more durable.

Horsehide Butt: Tanned into cordovan leather which makes extremely sturdy, durable, and highly polished shoe uppers.

Sheepskin (no wool): Thin and very strong. The best diplomas are made from vegetable-tanned sheepskin.

Goatskin: Thin and very fine grained.

Kidskin: Most suedes are kidskins (young goats) buffed on the flesh side. One of the sturdiest of leathers, kid is also one of the softest and most pliable.

Pigskin: Domestic pigskin is often pierced by hair follicles through the fat layer. For this reason, it is generally considered weak and inferior.

Peccary: Leather from the South American hog which is used for shoes, gloves, wallets, and luggage.

Deerskin: Soft, supple, and strong. Small skins, usually ragged and full of holes and scratches. Color almost always gold. Very expensive if purchased tanned.

Kangaroo: The strongest of all leathers. Used for track, baseball, and dress shoes.

Sharkskin: Leather for shoe uppers and small leather goods.

Some other terms you might need to be familiar with when purchasing leather include the following:

Suede: Fuzzy napped. Finished by buffing the flesh side to produce the surface texture. Not related to the skin type.

Sheepskin Suede: Fine-grained, small skins.

Garment Suede/Cowhide or Suede Splits: Cowhides commercially split to give two or more layers. The underside layer is treated to produce a fine, velvetlike surface. Comes in many thicknesses and colors. May or may not have both sides sueded (can have a suede side and a smooth side). Generally, suede from cowhide splits is weak and can tear under strain.

Doeskin: Made from sheep or lambskin with the hair removed.

Chamois: A product of oil-tanning the underneath layer ("flesher") that has been split from a sheepskin.

Latigo: Oil-tanned cowhide. Permanently soft, pliable, rot-resistant because of the oil content. Also a term applied to a type of retanned cowhide.

Rawhide: Not tanned. Special applications for mallets, drumheads, moccasin soles, and laces.

Sheep Shearling: Sueded on one side, wool on the other. The wool is usually trimmed to an even thickness and length of about ½ inch. Generally a brown or gold suede side and white or off-white wool but can be dyed any color.

Oak-Tanned Leather: Treated with tannic acid, usually obtained from vegetable materials. Stiff. Can be molded when wet and will keep its shape best of all leathers. Usually squeaks when it's rolled up. Darkens with age.

Chrome-Tanned Leather: Treated with chromium salts. Soft, floppy, and pliable. Garment use. Can be dyed any color.

Retanned Leather: Both oak and chrome tanned. Softer than oak-tanned, stiffer than chrome-tanned.

Stuffed Leather: Soaked in hot oil and/or wax.

Buck-Tanned Cowhide: Treated commercially to feel like buckskin made from deer hides. Soft, spongy, and feels somewhat stretchy. Usually has a suede side and can be dyed any color.

Leather thickness is measured in ounces (one ounce = $\frac{1}{64}$-inch thick) and calculated by the number of ounces per square foot weighed. Belting and tooling leather is usually six to twelve ounces; garment leather, two to nine ounces. Upholstery leather is similar in thickness to garment leather, but is heavier and stronger. Thus, this

Leather Thickness

used for clothing · linings
Hats · upholstery

2 - 3 ounce
2/64" to 3/64" thick

clothing · Zipper Gussets

3 - 4 ounce
3/64" to 4/64" thick

for slightly heavier articles
slippers · moccasins
Watch bands · Bracelets

4 - 5 ounce
4/64" to 5/64" thick

heavier weight for belts · Handbags
Straps

6 - 7 ounce
6/64 to 7/64 thick

Briefcases · Handbags · Belts

7 - 8 ounce
7/64" to 8/64 thick

Belts · Rifle Holsters · Saddle Bags
necklace pendants ·

8 - 9 ounce
8/64" to 9/64" thick

Carved Belts

9 - 10 ounce
9/64" to 10/64" thick

Carpenters Belts · Sandals

10 - 11 ounce
10/64" to 11/64" thick

measurement of thickness is not always a measurement of strength. For instance, pigskin at two to three ounces per square foot is stronger than calfskin, which is three to five ounces per square foot.

Most leathers sold commercially are separated according to quality. Keep in mind, however, that even top grades will have some blemishes. Tannery run (TR) hides are not graded and are generally less expensive.

Finally, when shopping for leather, remember that several common leather finishes are available: smooth, grained, waxy, patent, lustre, suede, and embossed. Leathers are finished in many ways commercially that the home tanner can never hope to duplicate.

If you are interested in sewing with furs, but don't tan your own, you may find that you do not have the ready access to tanned furskins that you do to leathers. Most leather stores sell tanned rabbit skins, but many don't even carry those. To purchase tanned furskins, you might have to go directly to a home tanner or a commercial tannery for your materials.

Whether you've tanned or purchased your leather or fur, you have the raw material that you'll need for hours of creative fun making exciting crafts and beautiful garments. Before you dive in and get started, there is one rule to remember when working with leather and fur:

Try new techniques on a scrap first.

Don't risk ruining an expensive piece of leather by jumping in and trying something with which you are unfamiliar. Techniques such as dyeing are not always as easy as they look, and you could benefit from a little practice before tackling the main project. Even such seemingly simple matters as hole-punching and stitching should be practiced on scraps before doing it on the pattern pieces.

Another valuable idea to use when sewing garments from leather or fur is to make a *muslin dummy*. This involves taking the pattern you intend to use with leather and making the garment in muslin or some other inexpensive cloth first. Muslin is usually used because it is readily available, cheap, has some body, and has no pattern or color to detract from the fit and line of the garment. Make sure the garment is roomy enough to avoid any pull or tension on the skins which might tear in high-stress areas. Also keep in mind that winter clothing such as coats and jackets must fit over heavy sweaters and other winter wear without pulling too much on the seams.

Hand Sewing

Most of the equipment and procedures discussed here are common to all leather and furwork since most leathers and furskins can be sewn by hand.

Leather needles are recommended for all hand sewing of leather and fur. These needles have three sharp, cutting edges at the point that leave a cleaner hole in the material. The largest size is #000 which is used for thick suedes and sheepskins. Don't use a large needle with thin leathers and furskins, however, as they leave too large a hole, and the thin leather could rip apart at the seams. The smaller-sized leather needles are called *glovers' needles* and are perfect for fur work.

Saddlers' needles are specialty leather needles that come straight and curved, generally in the larger sizes.

Thicker leather can also be handsewn, but usually holes are punched first and a dull-pointed *harness needle* is used for the stitching.

Don't use 100 percent cotton thread on leather articles, as it will usually rot and the article will fall apart at the seams. Several different thread types are excellent for use with leathers and furs:

Saddlers' Thread: Thick. Useful for heavy-duty leather articles.

Carpet and Button Thread: A good, all-purpose hand-sewing thread.

Waxed Linen Thread: Slides easily through the seams.

The illustration shows several handstitches commonly used with leathers and furs. These stitches are applicable to both needle-and-thread sewing as well as leather lacing through punched holes. Try to keep

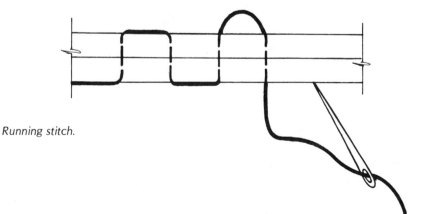

Running stitch.

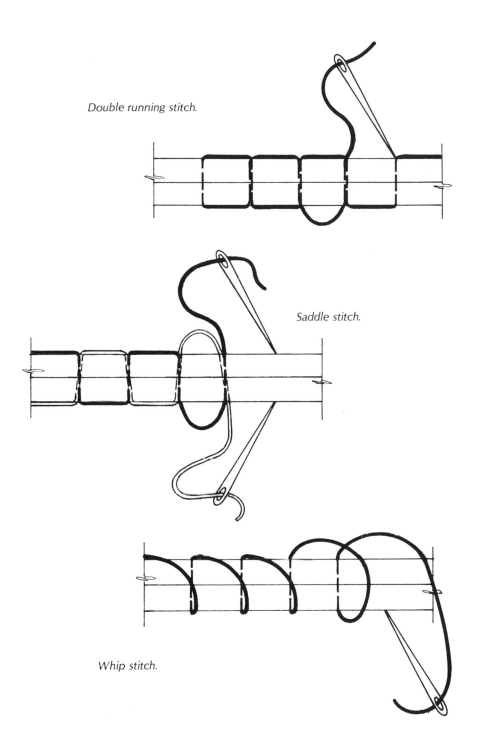

Double running stitch.

Saddle stitch.

Whip stitch.

your stitches as even and equally spaced as you can for the best appearance and strength. Handstitching can be done either from the inside for furs and a hidden seamline or from the outside as a decoration on leather items.

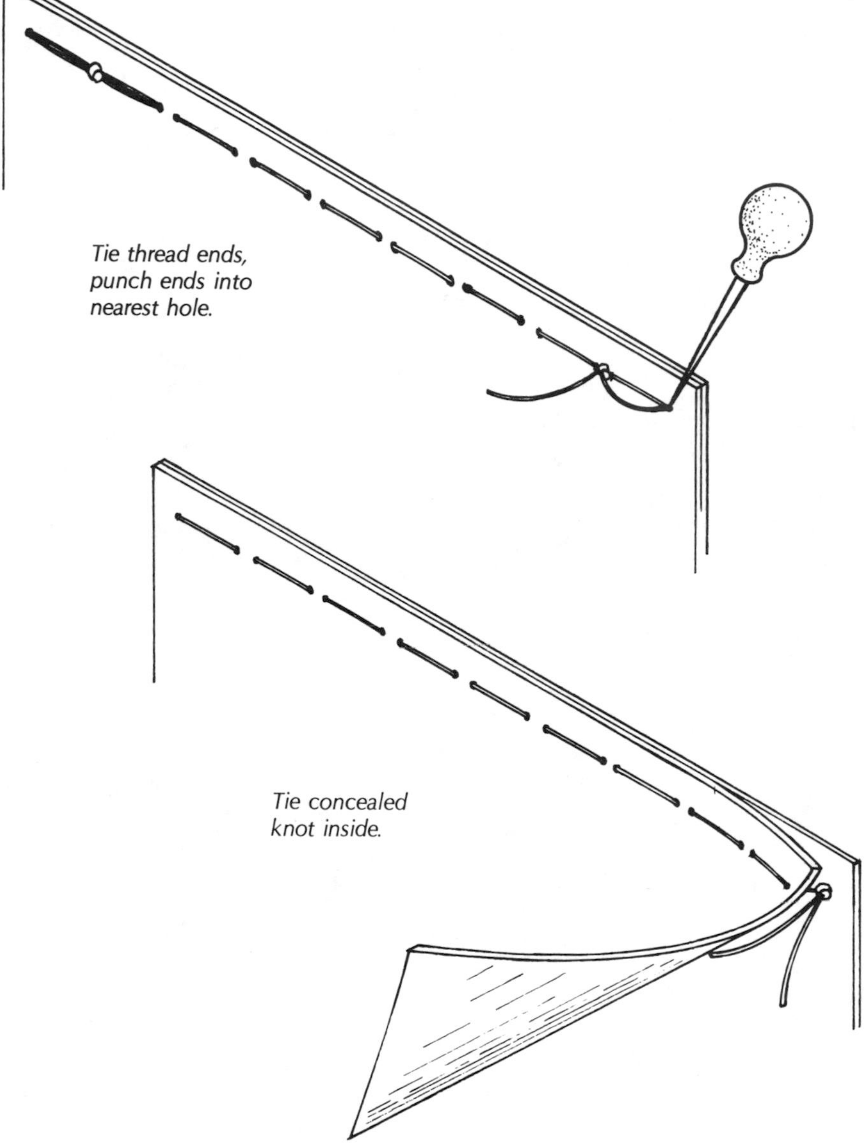

Ends . . . (thread).

Tie thread ends, punch ends into nearest hole.

Tie concealed knot inside.

The illustration shows ways to secure the thread ends of a hand-sewn seam. Lacing ends can be finished as shown in this illustration.

Ends . . . (lacing).

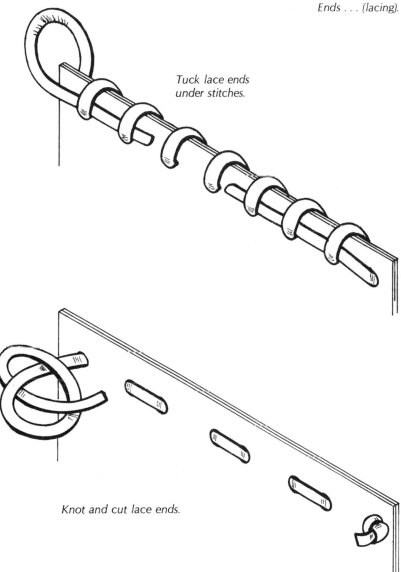

Tuck lace ends under stitches.

Knot and cut lace ends.

lapped seam —

under piece

rubber cement

over piece

stitching

gluing up a hem

rubber cement

hem

foldline

note: rubber cement stains leather. be sure to keep it within overlapped areas.

Many leather and fur items are glued together or have the seams glued down flat and the hems glued up. Rubber cement is the glue easiest to obtain for this purpose. It will not stiffen the leather, stain, or soak through to the front side. Furthermore, the leather pieces can be pulled up and repositioned before the cement has dried. Leather cement is more expensive and less readily available, but works the same way as rubber cement.

Machine Sewing

Many soft, thin leathers and furskins can be easily sewn with any good home sewing machine. A few machine adjustments and special techniques make machine sewing easier, but otherwise it's the same as sewing any relatively heavy cloth.

Because leather is thicker, softer, and more easily compressed than cloth, reduce the pressure exerted by the foot plate. See your machine instruction or service manual for the specific directions. It is best to loosen the pressure regulator as much as possible when sewing furskins.

Use the longest stitch possible (seven to nine stitches per inch). If you use closer stitching, the result will be a row of holes in the leather with much the same effect as a perforated line in paper; the garment will tear apart at the seams. Because of the bulkiness of the skins, the stitches will tend to be closer together than the setting indicates.

Set the stitch tension to achieve an even seam. The tension used for most fabrics is too high for leathers and furs. If the upper tension is too high, the upper thread will pull the bobbin thread to the top surface. If it's too low, the bobbin will pull the upper thread to the bottom. Use some leather or fur scraps and two different colors of bobbin and upper threads to adjust the tension until it is even with only the bobbin thread showing on the bottom and only the upper thread on the top.

Use a medium-sized sewing machine needle. If the needle is too small and thin, it won't be able to penetrate the leather and will probably break. A needle that is too large makes a hole that is too big and visable.

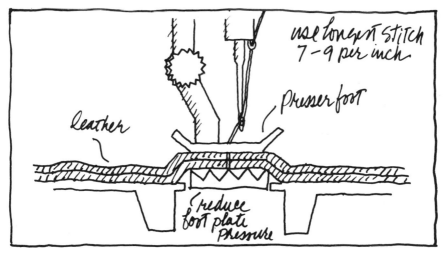

Specialty attachments for sewing skins are helpful, but not necessary. A roller or teflon-coated presser foot will help the leather slide through without sticking. Leather sewing machine needles similar to glovers' needles in a medium size give a cleaner, more easily pierced hole. These items are generally available from sewing machine sales and service stores.

Hairhides (leather with the hair left on), furskins, and glossy-finished leathers are the most difficult to sew by machine because the two layers slip easily when faced together to be sewn. Use paper clips or long, thin pins to hold the layers together, and sew the seam slowly. Also, steady pulling will often help get the leather through the machine without the layers sticking or sliding apart. Or tape the sewing edges with masking or duct tape along the stitching line. This taping will also help strengthen the seam.

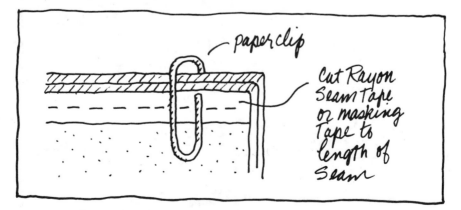

Don't backstitch seams when sewing leather or fur by machine, as this will weaken the seam because of the many holes. Secure seam ends by knotting the ends together.

To reinforce seams on which there will be a great deal of strain, such as pockets and shoulders, double stitch, placing one seam approximately $\frac{1}{8}$-$\frac{1}{16}$-inch away from the other. Seam binding or tape along the seam line also helps.

Despite popular beliefs, small bits of fur that get into your sewing machine when working with furskins will not harm it. But to be on the safe side, clean your machine after every sewing session. You should get in the habit of doing this to extend the life of the sewing machine and improve its performance.

If you don't own a sewing machine or would like to invest in one designed for fur, a fur-sewing machine is available. It is very expensive, but does a tiny overcast stitch on the very edge of the seam. It's not necessary for pelts such as rabbit, and is mostly used for expensive, fragile skins such as mink and chinchilla.

Another sewing machine type is the heavy, industrial power machine. Its main advantage is that it's fast. This can be very handy when doing a large item like a bedspread that has lots of long, straight seams. But all that speed is not needed and can be a disadvantage for most fur and leather garments with their many short, often curved seams. If you would like to use a power machine for a large project, you can rent one.

One final suggestion before you begin your leather or fur item: much of the procedure, especially with garment leathers and furs, is the same as constructing a garment from fabric. However, don't try to apply all the rules of fabric construction when working with leathers. Use your common sense. For instance, don't try to iron seams to flatten them as you would with cloth. Leather and furs are treated differently. To flatten and secure seams and hems, use rubber cement to hold the seam or hem in place. Then cover with a warm, damp cloth and flatten the seam or hemline with a few blows from a wooden mallet.

Take your time, use your common sense, and you will have a leather or fur garment or craft item that you will be proud of for years!

Some tools and materials needed for leatherwork.
1. De-haired rabbit leather (from a mature, thick-skinned buck rabbit).
2. Belt buckles. 3. Oak-tanned cowhide strips used for belts.
4. Leather dye and finish. 5. Leather lacing. 6. Revolving punch.
7. Edge beveler. 8. Packet of rivets.

chapter 7

Elementary Leatherwork

Tools and Materials

Hundreds of different leather tools are available on the market but most beginners can get by with only a few. A leather or utility knife, hole punch or awl, and mallet are probably the bare minimum. Those and a large, sturdy, and preferably damage-proof worktable are all the leathercrafter needs besides the standard needles and thread or lacing. However, owning and using some of the more sophisticated leather tools make the job infinitely more enjoyable and far easier.

The most dangerous tool you will use is the *leather knife.* Use it with the same care you give your skinning knife: keep it sharp and only use it for its intended purpose. Keep your fingers out of the track of the blade when cutting. Hold the knife in your right hand, if you are right-handed, and use your left hand to hold the leather in place behind the knife, if possible. A *leather shears* is a much safer alternative to the knife, but also more expensive. Small pieces, fringe, or laces can be cut with an X-Acto knife or razor blade, using the same precautions as with the leather knife, always cutting away from the hand holding the blade

Leather Knife: best for cutting Thick leathers

Moisten leather before cutting

Hold rule down firmly to avoid slippage

Steel rule

and never hurrying. Heavier leather is often easier to cut with a knife or razor blade if you moisten the leather with water before cutting.

Most leather is too thick to be sewn directly by hand, so holes are punched and a blunt needle is used to stitch through the holes. *Hole punches* come in a variety of types and sizes. A *thonging punch* makes

Leather Shears: serrated edges prevent slippage by holding leather Best for cutting lighter weight leather holes for sewing with thread. An *awl-type punch* is used with a mallet and a hard sole-leather backing because punching against wood or stone will blunt the tip.

The most popular, easiest to use punch is the *revolving punch* which has six or more different hole sizes and is used like a pliers or scissors. The smallest hole size is used for thread, the medium sizes for rivets and snaps, and the largest for lacing and thongs. When working with leathers, punch one layer at a time. Mark the location of the holes on the first layer and punch them first. Then mark the back of the second layer through the holes in the first layer and punch them.

Rotary Punch with interchangable heads makes round holes for lacings and snaps

4 in 1 Round Hole Punch for leathers up to 5 ounces

For most leather projects, you must thin the edges of the leather either for a better appearance or to reduce the bulk. *Edge bevelers* and *skiving knives* are used for this. They come in a wide variety of sizes to match different leather thicknesses. Skiving is shaving the back side of a piece of leather to make it more flexible or to reduce seam bulk. A little leather at a time is removed until it is thin enough. Beveling is similar in many ways to skiving, but is usually applied to the upper or front side as well as the back of a thick piece of leather, such as a belt, to round the sharp edge.

Skiving with a leather knife

skiver

Cutting a Pattern

Most patterns designed for fabric can be used to make garments from buckskin, suede, or thin garment leather. It is usually wise to make a muslin dummy of the pattern to check for fit before cutting from leather. You will need to add ¼-½ inch to the seam allowance and sleeve and leg hems when using commercial clothing patterns with leather, as leather garments should fit more loosely than fabric ones. Remember that you can always take a garment in if it's too large, but it's difficult to make it bigger if you cut it too small.

As a guideline, you will need the following amounts of leather to make these garments and crafts items:

Jackets and coats	30-40 square feet
Gloves and moccasins	3 square feet
Handbag	3-6 square feet

Don't fold the leather and try to cut two layers at once, regardless of the pattern directions. When using cloth, folding and cutting is often possible and recommended, but leather has a tendency to slip and the pattern may not be cut evenly. Also, you cannot see where the scars and flaws are on the underside if you cut two pieces at once. Use only full-sized pattern pieces cut one at a time.

Scar-dodging is important to conserve leather and to avoid blemishes that could show on the finished piece. Scars and other flaws may overlap into the pattern slightly in the seam allowance, but they must not occur in the seam line. A scar, even on the backside, is a weak spot in the leather, is usually hard to sew through, and could rip out.

When cutting patterns, it is usually easier and safer to trace or outline the pattern on the back side of the leather. That way, mistakes or pattern adjustments will not show on the finished side.

A special way to cut leather to make a little bit go a long way is called *expanded leather*. The skin is cut in such a way that it forms a netlike structure. It is used for projects where strength is not required, such as purses, hats, and plant hangers. Each cut has a little hole punched in each end with an awl or a small punch to prevent tearing of the leather. Vary the width of the strips and uncut areas according to the strength of the leather used.

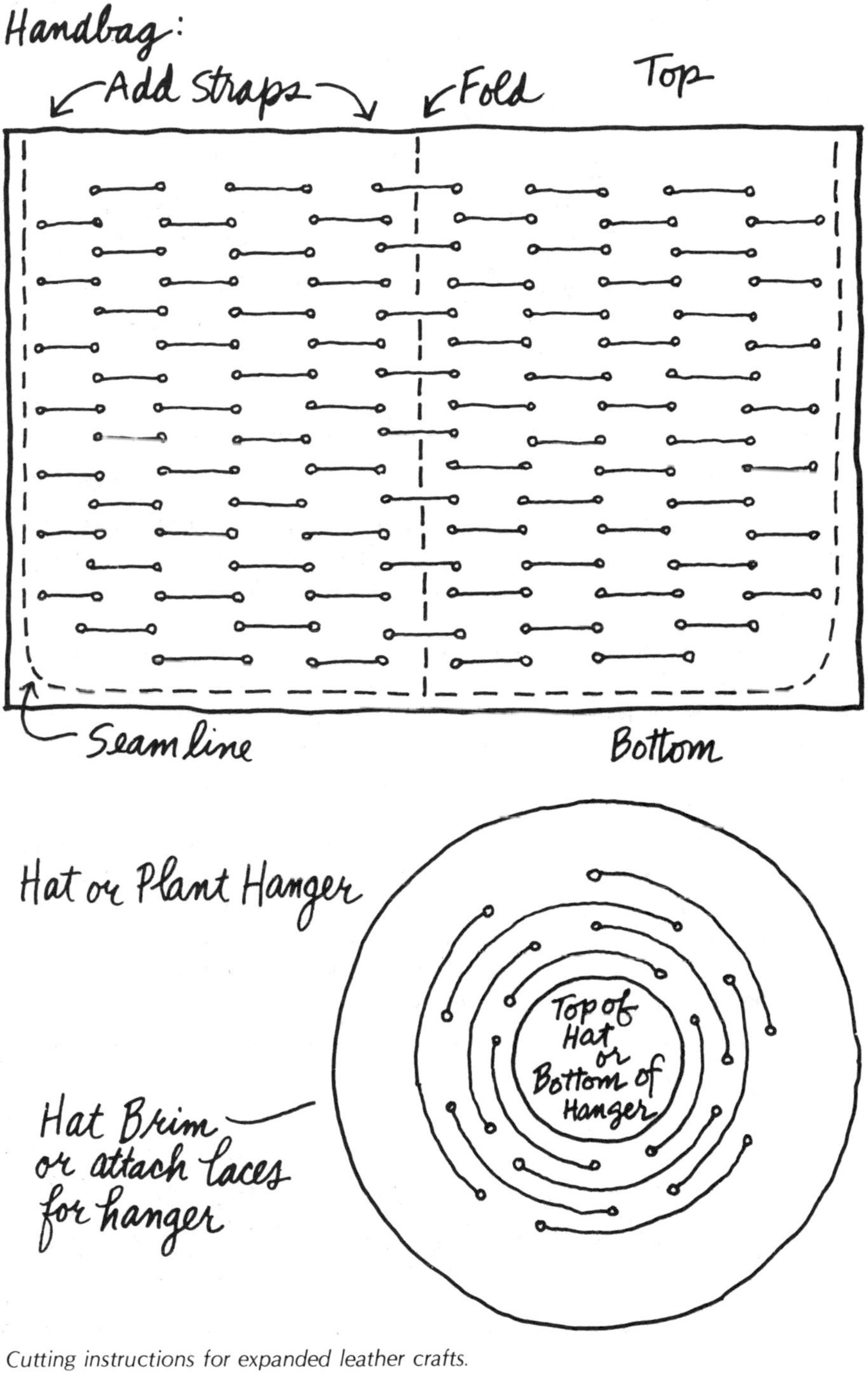

Handbag:

Add Straps → ← Fold   Top

← Seam line   Bottom

Hat or Plant Hanger

Top of
Hat
or
Bottom of
Hanger

Hat Brim
or attach laces
for hanger

Cutting instructions for expanded leather crafts.

Keep hand firm on work Table to make a steady cut

Tooling

Tooling is basically leather carving. Many different knives and stamp patterns are available from leather supply stores. Only vegetable-tanned leathers, four or more ounces in thickness, can be successfully tooled.

To carve leather, you need a hard surface, preferably one of marble, and a wooden or rawhide mallet. A swivel knife cuts in the patterns, a beveler "raises" them. Cutting a dry leather surface produces a shallow cut; wet surface carving produces a deeper cut. When wetting leather, dampen (don't soak) the entire surface with a sponge, even if you only want to tool a small area, to prevent water spotting.

Stamping designs is always done on dampened leather. Stamps are available in hundreds of designs, from the letters of the alphabet to zodiac signs. The stamp's imprint is permanently carved into the damp leather by hitting the stamp against the hide with a mallet.

Dyes and lacquers enhance carved and stamped designs as well as firming and protecting the leather.

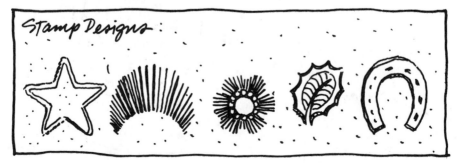

Stamp Designs:

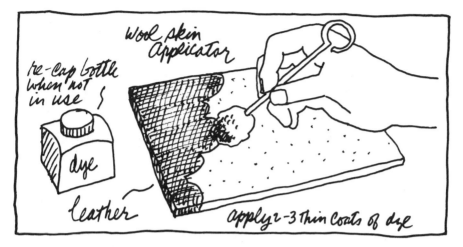

Re-cap bottle when not in use

Wool skin Applicator

dye

leather

apply 2-3 Thin Coats of dye

Dyeing

All coloring should be done after cutting and usually after tooling, but before assembly. Several dyes especially designed for leather are available from leather or crafts stores. Most soft garment leathers and buckskin types are dyed commercially during or after the tanning process. You shouldn't attempt dyeing large garment leather skins yourself, as it is extremely difficult to get the color even.

Most oak-tanned leathers, which are used for many items such as belts, handbags, and saddles, are dyed or colored or at least have finishes applied. Dampening oak-tanned leather before applying the dye helps the coloring to penetrate better. Sanding roughens the surface of the leather, accentuating the grain and permitting the dye to penetrate easier as well. Use only #100-200 grade sandpaper, which is very fine.

Follow the instructions on the leather dye you are using. Many have a volatile petroleum base and should be applied with caution. Use in a well-ventilated area, with plenty of newspapers under the leather if the workspace is not damage-proof. Recap the bottle when it is not in use. Spills happen all too frequently.

Most dyes are applied with clean, lint-free rags or woolskin applicators. Two or three thin coats give a better finish than one heavy one. Let the coloring dry between coats.

Acrylic finishes are an alternative to coloring. They don't change the leather's color, but they bring out the grain and darken the beveled edges and tooling designs. These finishes usually have a wax and a sealer, and can be buffed to a glossy shine after drying. Most can be used on dyed leather as well. Again, follow the instructions on the product you are using.

Assembling

Stitching and Lacing

In sewing most leathers, you'll have to punch holes before stitching. Large, thick lacing (about ³⁄₁₆ inch wide) needs holes ½ inch apart. Thinner lacing, usually made of calfskin and about ⅛ inch wide, requires five holes to the inch. The length of lacing required for a given project depends on the hole spacing as well as how tightly you pull the laces. But, based on the given hole spacing suggestions above, use the following lengths:

 Running stitch—1½ times as long as the seam

 Whipstitch—3½ times as long as the seam

 Double running or saddle stitch—3 times as long as the seam

When in doubt, use extra lacing. It's easier to cut off a little at the end than to add more if you run short. Putting paraffin, beeswax, or old candle wax on the lacing and using a special lacing needle make the job easier and faster. Pull the ends snug as you go on each stitch and finish the ends as shown in the illustration.

Hand sewing seams in thinner leathers on the outside looks more professional if the location of the stitches is marked before sewing to insure even spacing. Special tools are available for this purpose, but a simple kitchen fork marks evenly spaced dots showing where the stitches should be.

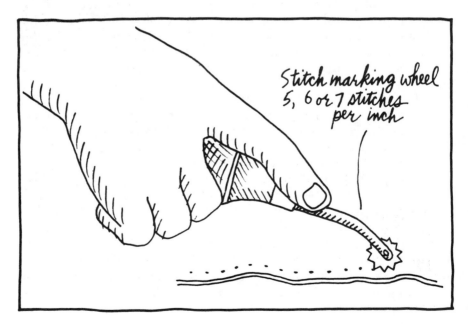

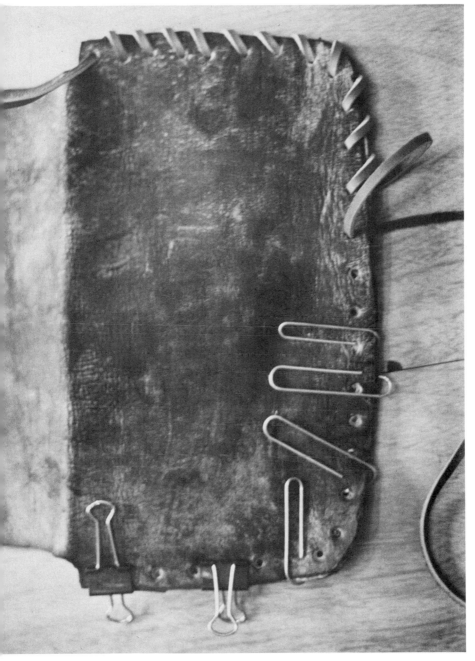

Lacing together a simple wallet with a whipstitch.

Rivets and Snaps

Both rivets and snaps come in a variety of sizes for different leather thicknesses. A rivet fastens two pieces of leather together permanently and is best used for relatively small areas. Snaps are used for similar applications, but the two pieces of leather can be separated.

Leatherworking rivets have two parts, a top and a bottom. They are fastened together by hammering the top piece to the bottom on a metal block using the following sequence of steps:

1. Punch medium holes in the two pieces of leather that you wish to rivet together.

2. Stand the bottom of the rivet on the metal block.

3. Place the leather holes over the rivet bottom. Make sure that the bottom piece of leather is on the bottom. It's very difficult to remove the rivet and do it over if you mistakenly have the rivet bottom where the top should be.

4. Fit the rivet top over the rivet bottom, through the leather holes.

5. Set the rivet by hammering with a mallet or rivet set punch.

Rivets are used most commonly for fastening leather around a belt buckle, to fasten straps onto purses and handbags, and for high stress connections.

Snaps are a little trickier. They are usually four-part and are attached to the leather with a special tool which either comes with the snaps or is purchased separately.

Gluing

Rubber cement is the easiest, cheapest, and most readily available glue for leatherworking (see the Introduction to Part III for more information).

To use rubber cement to attach two pieces of leather, rough up the sections to be glued with fine sandpaper. Then apply a thin, even layer of cement to both surfaces. Wait ten to twenty minutes until the cement is tacky. Then press the two surfaces together and secure by pounding lightly with a wooden or rawhide mallet. Gluing is useful for flattening seams, putting up hems, and attaching facings before lining.

PROJECT: Leather Belt, Wristbands or Dog Collars

Belts, bands, and collars are essentially long strips of leather (seven to ten-ounce, oak-tanned belting and tooling types work best) cut parallel to the animal's spine for the greatest strength. Such strips are available, precut and often pre-punched, in leather supply stores. Use a yardstick to draw straight lines when cutting your own.

Before you choose or cut your leather, choose a buckle. Buckles come in three basic types: harness, strap and hook, and center bar.

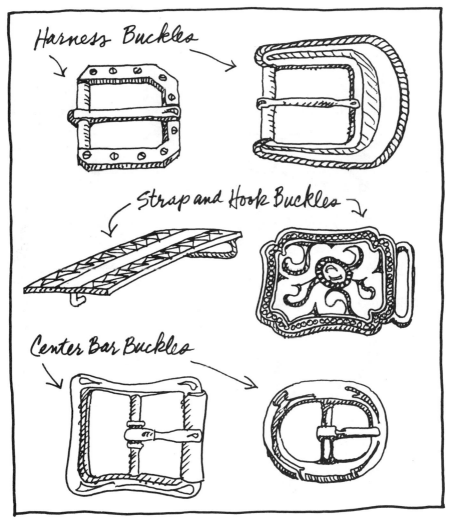

Buckle types.

Next, purchase or cut a strip of leather to fit the buckle. For a belt, the leather should be 7½ to 8 inches longer than your waist measurement. Add five to six inches for other bands and dog collars. This extra length allows for fastening the belt around the buckle and for buckle holes.

Bevel the edges, front and back, of the leather strip. Next, trim the point that will go through the buckle. Rounded is best, as sharp points tend to curl up with use. Bevel this end, too.

Then punch medium holes for the buckle prong or hood on the trimmed end. Punch at least three holes, one inch apart and 1½ inches from the belt end.

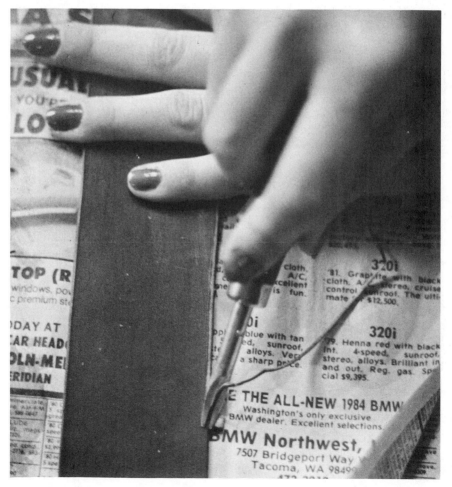

Bevelling the edges of a belt strip.

Punch the buckle prong/hook holes.

Applying dye to the leather belt strip.

Punch rivet or snap holes as shown in the illustration. For strap and hood buckles, omit the center hole for the buckle prong. This elongated hole can be made either with a special oblong punch or by punching a series of round holes to create the oblong. If you rivet the buckle to the belt, the leather will have to be cut to change buckles. Snaps permit using many buckles on the same belt and, hence, are often preferred.

Tool or dye the leather after beveling, punching, and trimming, but before attaching the buckle. Use an acrylic finish or neutral shoe wax to buff up, shine, and protect the surface after the dye is dry.

Location of rivet/snap holes.

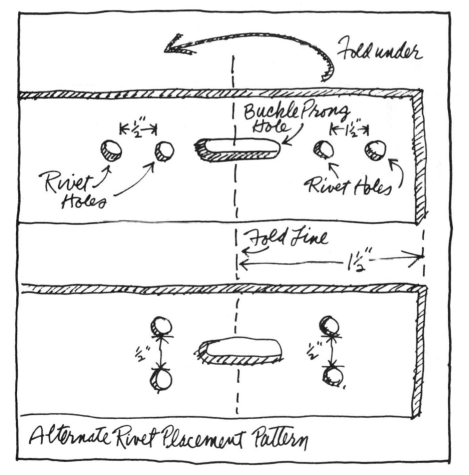

Attach the buckle to the belt as shown in the illustration. The little loop of leather that holds the point of the belt down after it goes through the buckle is called a *keeper*. Fasten the keeper to the belt with rivets or snaps after the buckle is attached. Your belt is now ready to be used. Additional holes can be punched if the size needs to be adjusted at some later date. Keep your new leather belt shiny and new-looking by occasionally reapplying acrylic finish or shoe wax and buffing with a lint-free cloth.

Buckle attachment.

Two belts, before and after buckle attachment.

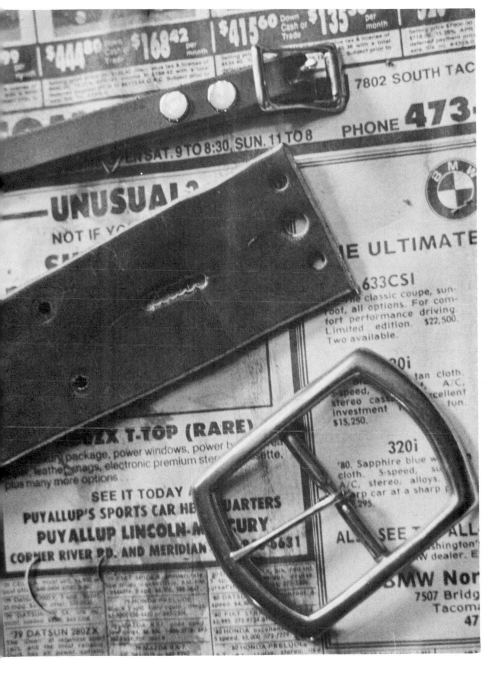

Footwear Primer

The history of shoemaking in the United States is closely allied with the meat-production and tanning industries. Nearly 80 percent of all the leather produced in this country goes into the manufacture of shoes. Until 1850, nearly all the steps in the shoemaking process were done by hand. Today, there are almost 10,000 machine and tool patents for shoemaking equipment.

One of the chief virtues of leather for shoes is that it permits the shoe to mold itself to the shape of the wearer's foot, thus providing maximum support and comfort. Also, leather breathes and so can the feet, lessening the chances of foot ailments caused by other shoe materials.

Making shoes by hand is an art that takes both time and skill. If you are interested in trying your hand at it, hunt up a copy of the book *Shoes For Free People* by David and Inger Runk. I will only attempt to give you a brief overview of the process in this book.

MATERIALS: You will need sole leather (vegetable tanned preferred); bottom or upper leather, not heavier than four or five ounces (should be a soft oil or vegetable tanned leather. Seven to ten pairs of shoes can be cut from one entire steer hide); and hard rubber for the heels.

TOOLS AND SUPPLIES: A *last* is a wooden or plastic form shaped like a human foot used for making shoes. It's especially useful when making many pairs of shoes in an "average" size. However, if you are interested in making only shoes for yourself or some other person who will be around for measurements, it is infinitely better to use a real foot as a form.

Cinching nails or sole nails are special for shoe manufacture. The nails pass through the layers of leather and bend over at the point. They are used to fasten the layers of the soles together. The art of driving the nails with a small hammer against a steel block, alternating from top to bottom, is called *cobbling* and hence shoemakers earned the name cobblers.

Besides the foot form and nails, you will need harness needles, harness awl, glue ruffler or sandpaper, rubber cement, a cobbler's hammer, leather shears and/or a leather knife, leather rasp, pliers, stitching spacer, calipers, a revolving hole punch, and possibly other tools. You can see by the amount of equipment that shoemaking is not a task to be entered into lightly.

Leather Care

Footwear

Saddle soap is sometimes recommended as best for leather shoes. Boots can be made water-resistant by occasional applications of neat's-foot oil or snowproofing grease. Oil and grease make the color of the shoes darker, but they will also keep your feet dry. Don't use products that contain silicon on shoes or other leather products, as they will tend to crack the leather.

Suede and Split Leather

Suede leather seldom needs dry-cleaning if it is brushed regularly with a towel to keep dust from settling in the nap. This dust is shed by the new suede leather. Most spots and stains can be removed by a soft eraser, emery board, or chalk-type cleaner, which usually comes in spray cans or sticks. Heavily soiled suede should be dry-cleaned. If suede gets wet, dry away from heat. Rub with a towel after drying to restore the original appearance.

Smooth and Grained Leather

Smooth leather may be cleaned with a damp cloth and mild soap, and then patted dry. Avoid detergents, cleaning fluids, and shoe creams. Dry a wet garment away from heat on a wooden or covered hanger.

To hang out wrinkles, leave the garment in a damp room overnight or press with a cool iron using heavy paper as a pressing cloth. Store in a well-ventilated closet in cloth or paper bags (not plastic) to prevent the accumulation of dust.

A pair of home-grown rabbit fur coats.

chapter 8

Sewing
with
Fur

Fur work is more properly considered in the realm of the furrier, not the leatherworker, because the techniques of the fur industry are more similar to clothesmaking and tailoring than to those of the leather craftsperson. The fur industry is still largely a handicraft enterprise with most of the trade being in handmade items. However, 90 percent of all commercial fur garments, mainly coats and jackets, are manufactured in only a few square blocks of New York City. Nonetheless, furs are available in all parts of the world, with the most valuable coming from northernmost regions such as Canada, Alaska, and Siberia.

In the industry, pelts are grouped by class and graded for primeness. Class A furs include mink, chinchilla, seal, beaver, sable, nutria, fox, and Russian broadtail. Class B includes all other furs except Class C, which includes only rabbit and mouton. Most commercial furs, sold green-dried, are dressed by tanneries before being made into high-priced fur garments. Dressing includes all the tanning, shearing, pulling, and dyeing operations.

The modern farmsteader and trapper doesn't need to pay outrageous sums of money if he or she desires the warmth, comfort, and beauty of fur items. Making your own clothing from furskins is not overly difficult if you have a working knowledge of sewing techniques. Working with the thin leather of fur pelts is much the same as working with thick, nappy fabric. Anyone who sews should be able to make the transition from fabric to fur.

The first step is to decide what you want to make and then to choose a pattern. Matching pelts for color, density, and texture is important if you wish to make any article of clothing and avoid patchiness. This list shows the number of skins needed to complete a few projects. This is approximate; the number depends somewhat on skin size and quality.

Items	Skins
Mink coat:	65 to 85
Mink jacket:	about 45
Full-length rabbit coat:	40 to 50
Rabbit jacket:	16 to 24
Mink stole:	10 to 25
Large rabbit stole:	14 to 18
22-inch rabbit cape:	14 to 18
Medium rabbit vest:	8 to 10
Short rabbit cape or a small rabbit stole:	7 to 10
Rabbit fur-lined mittens or slippers:	2 to 4
4-foot by 5-foot rabbit bedspread or lap rug:	25 to 35
Rabbit fur pillow:	2 to 8
Large rabbit fur purse:	4

The best part of any furskin is a rectangular portion in the center, along the spine. The fur at the neck tends to be thinner and shorter and the belly pieces are often less durable and attractive.

Matching Pelts

Before matching pelts for a project, stitch up small, even rips in the skin with a small overcast or whipstitch on the skin side. Then mark molty patches, hairslip areas, unhealed wounds, and noticeable scars by pushing a ballpoint pen or dull harness needle into the skin from the fur side all around the damaged area. When you turn the pelt over to the skin side, you will see a little circle of bumps around all the bad areas. Circle these bumpy circles with a felt-tip or wax marking pen. You can also mark off the thin, short belly and neck areas this way.

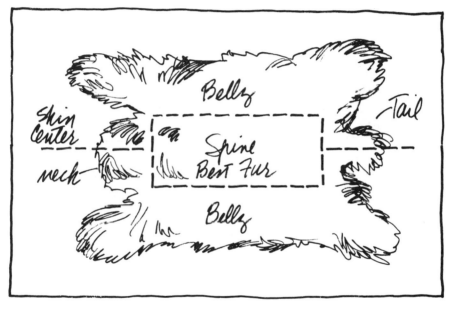

Match color, density, and length of the furs by laying the pelts fur side up together on a large table. Examine them closely, blowing into the fur and rubbing it with your hand. Group the matching pelts together.

If you are working with a large pattern piece, such as a coat, or you want to make a patchwork coverlet or lap robe, square-mark all the pelts you will be using by drawing a straight line at the neck, tail and both belly sections. The areas beyond the lines will be trimmed away and the squares or rectangles sewn together into one large piece before laying out your pattern. Keep the squares the same size and the fur going in one direction by attaching necks to rumps and bellies to bellies, unless you want to achieve a special fur effect by mixing fur directions.

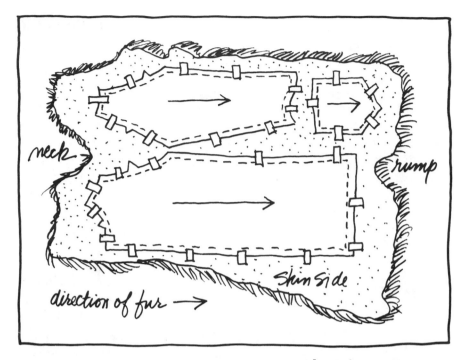

neck

rump

Skin Side

direction of fur ➝

Choosing a Pattern

Pick a pattern with simple lines for ease of construction and so that the fur will provide the interest rather than the line.

Raglan sleeves are better and easier to sew than set-in ones. Also, there is less stress at the shoulder area where seams are likely to rip out.

Button-buttonhole and zipper closures need a fabric or leather panel in front or the fur will bald in short order because of the amount of friction at these points. Hooks and eyes or belts make better closures when sewing garments with fur.

Any pattern designed for fabric, especially fake fur, can be adapted for use with fur. You can use a commercial tissue-paper variety of pattern or you can make your own pattern by cutting a full-sized paper pattern for each piece to be cut. If you are at all unsure about the fit of the finished garment, make a muslin dummy with the pattern before cutting into the pelts. Remember to allow extra room in the sleeves and body with fur coats and jackets because the garment will probably be worn over heavy winter clothing and because fur and leather garments should be somewhat larger than the fabric variety to lessen stress at the seams.

Cutting Furskins

The next step is to lay your pattern pieces on the skin sides of the pelts or on the *plate* made from several squared skins sewn together. Move the pieces around several times to avoid objectionable spots and to use the best pelt sections. Lay the pattern "with the grain" ("grain" runs from neck to rump) so that the fur nap of the finished item is running in the same direction as it did when it was on the animal.

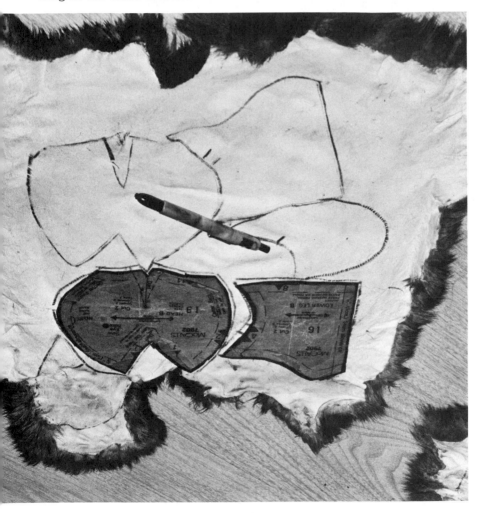

Marking pattern pieces onto the skin side of a rabbit pelt. Note how the pattern arrangement conserves the best fur section along the backbone.

Use tape, long pins, or small dots of rubber cement to hold the pattern pieces to the pelts when you have decided on the best arrangement. Allow only ⅛-¼-inch seam allowances with fur items to prevent bulk at the seam lines and to conserve fur. Trace the pattern pieces, and all instructions such as darts, onto the skin with a ballpoint, felt-tip, or wax marking pen. You can cut around each pattern piece without marking, but this is harder and less accurate.

The commercial fur industry works patterns in another way. Workers stretch the wetted furskin over patterns marked on wooden boards. When the pelt is dry, the excess is trimmed off.

The object when cutting furskins is to cut the skin but not the hair. Keeping the pelt area being cut above or lifted up from the cutting surface helps. Also, a leather knife, utility knife, or sharp razor blade won't cut as many hairs as a scissors. I have found that sharp shears can be used if you slowly snip only the skin along the pattern line, being extra careful not to make any long, deep cuts.

Not cutting the fur when cutting out the pattern assures that the seam line will be well covered in the finished garment. To decrease the bulk and bulge of the seam line further, you can trim the long fur close to the skin in the seam allowances with a small, sharp scissors.

No matter how careful you are or how hard you try to avoid it, expect some fur to fly when cutting furskins. It seems to be unavoidable to some extent. Therefore, keep your furrier work limited to one, easy-to-clean area. Have a paper sack on hand for scraps and bits of fur. You can use this "waste" later.

Plugging Holes

Sometimes you have a furskin that is prime and beautiful except for one small section of hairslip or a wound. Such areas can be patched if you wish to make use of this pelt. However, the process is not simple and the skin will never be as good as one that was totally prime.

First, mark the area to be removed using the "bump method" previously discussed. Keep in mind that horizontal lines will be more noticeable in the patch than vertical ones and that curves are harder to sew than straight lines.

Find another skin or a scrap of fur that matches the color and texture to use as the patch. It has to be large enough to cover the area being patched and to allow for a narrow seam.

Cut out the damaged area, carefully avoiding cutting hairs. Use the hole to make a pattern for the patch, adding about a $\frac{1}{16}$-inch seam allowance. Mark and cut out the patch.

Carefully sew the patch into the hole from the skin side by hand. This procedure cannot be accomplished on the machine. Put a warm, damp cloth over the patched area and flatten the seam with a wooden or rawhide mallet. Brush the fur in all directions to blend the patch hair with that of the pelt. Now you can use the patched skin either as part of a plate or for pattern pieces.

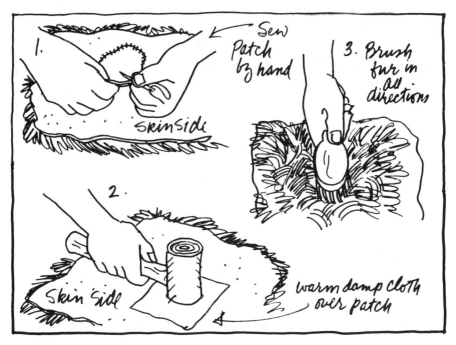

Sewing with Fur

Furskins can be sewn by hand or machine, as the leather is usually thin and easily pierced. Follow the directions that come with your pattern for assembly by hand or machine. A few suggestions will make the process easier, however, as fur work is a bit different from working with fabric.

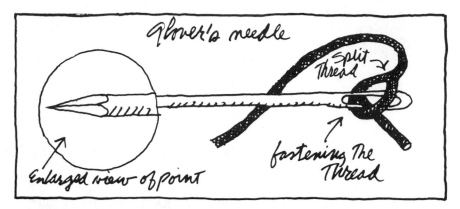

Hand Sewing: Sew from the skin side, as the thread can pick up hairs from the fur side, pulling them through the hole or causing an irritating knot. Use a glovers' needle and strong thread, pulling each stitch snugly. Keep your stitches fairly close together to avoid tearing out later and use a narrow whipstitch, overcasting the edges.

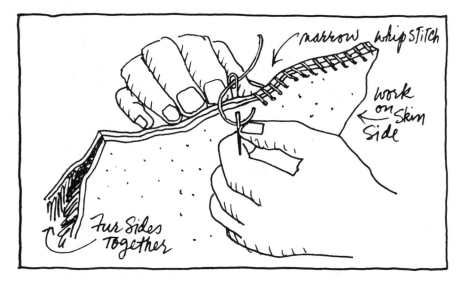

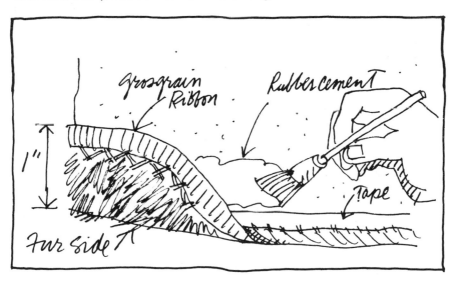

Seams: Hold pieces together for sewing with long, thin quilting pins, paper clips, or spring clips. Match and mark all seam lines at two-inch intervals when clipping the pattern pieces together. Leather sometimes sticks or slips when sewing by machine. Hence, the upper pattern piece may turn out shorter than a bottom piece stretched by sticking. If you mark the seams and keep an eye on the matching of the marks, you can correct for any stretching before you get to the end of the seam and find one piece an inch or more longer than the other.

Hems: The bottom edge of a garment can be finished with grosgrain ribbon or hem facing, or it can be left plain. It won't fray. You can either glue the hem and pound with a mallet to secure and flatten it, or you can hand sew it to the inside. You won't need as much hem allowance as suggested for fabric. A one-inch hem is usually plenty.

Joining Fur to Fabric or Soft Leather: Cut a full ⅝-inch seam allowance for fabric and ¼-inch for leather. Cut a narrow ¼-⅛-inch seam allowance for the fur. Put the fur pattern piece on top of the fabric or leather piece, matching seams, and sew on the seam line. Flatten the fur side of the seam with a damp cloth and mallet. Flatten the leather in this manner as well. The fabric can be flattened with a heated iron, being careful not to iron over the fur, since it burns easily.

Easing: It is simple to ease in fullness in a sleeve or other connection with fur because it can be stretched, pushed, and compressed on the skin side while you are sewing. Watch the seam to make sure you end up evenly.

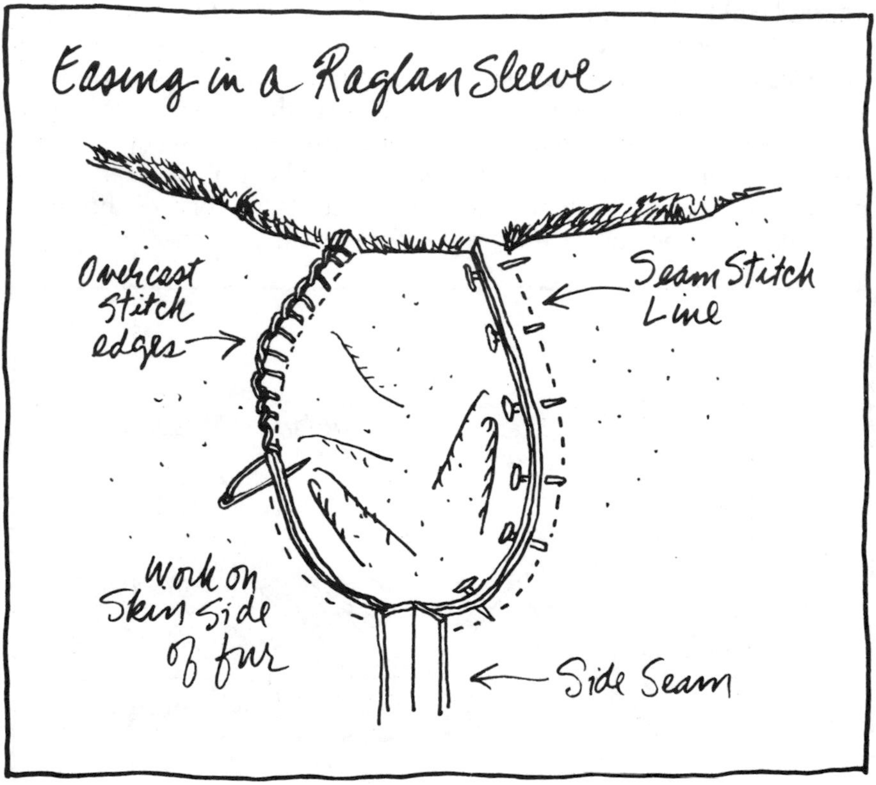

Easing in a Raglan Sleeve

Overcast Stitch edges →

← Seam Stitch Line

Work on Skin Side of fur

← Side Seam

Darts: Choose a vertical dart whenever possible. The horizontal dart often leaves an unattractive line in the fur. Cut out the middle of the dart after it is sewn. Flatten with a damp cloth and mallet and brush the dart line, freeing any trapped hairs. This will eliminate any excess bulk and streamline the area.

Pockets: Choose a pouch or inside pocket rather than a patch or outside pocket. It is less noticeable, does not detract from the line of the garment, and is far easier to sew.

Findings: Garment closures used on furs usually consist of crocheted hooks, eyes, and rings. These are available from fabric stores in a wide range of colors from black and white to browns and beiges to match nearly any fur.

Lining: Use the same procedures you would use with fabric. Make the fur part of the garment first, then make the lining section. Interlining, using a second lining attached to the inside of the main lining, is often used to prevent the skin from rubbing holes in the lining. Attach the lining to the fur by hand sewing at the neck area, sleeves, front facings, and possibly hems.

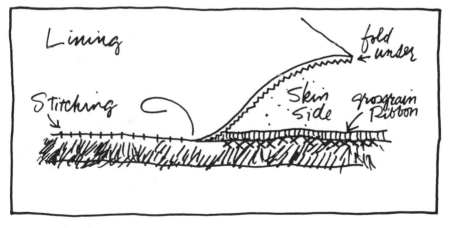

   To finish your creation, brush the fur side well with a fur brush or small hairbrush, paying particular attention to the joining lines such as seams, darts, and pockets. Free hairs trapped in these lines with a long needle.

PROJECT: Fur-lined Mittens

Pattern: To make a mitten pattern, trace around the wearer's hand. It is best to have the fingers at least partially spread to allow plenty of room in the mitten. Use heavy paper, such as grocery sacks, and a felt-tip marking pen. When tracing the hand, allow a ¼-inch seam allowance and ¾-inch spread allowance to keep the final mittens from being too tight. Hence, you will be cutting one inch total beyond the person's fingertips. Either mark the pattern one inch beyond the hand or trace the hand exactly and then add the one-inch allowance. You can extend the pattern from the widest part of the hand to the wrist or an inch or two up the arm. Make sure that the opening is at least wide enough to slip the hand into. Better too wide than not wide enough. Cut out your pattern.

Tracing a mitten pattern.

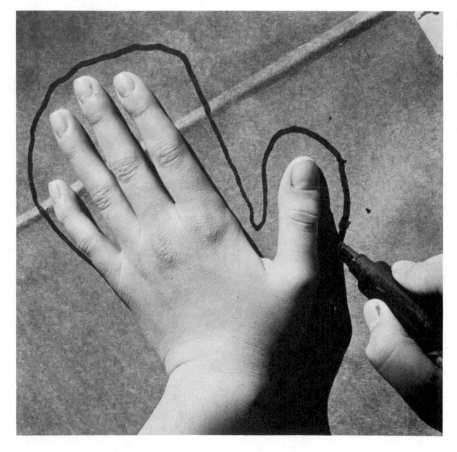

Materials needed for the mitten project, not including the fur skins.
1) Mitten pattern.   2) Ski-jacket material.
3) Knitted cuffs.   4) Heavy thread.
5) Long quilting pins to hold the pattern pieces together for sewing.
6) Glovers' needles.

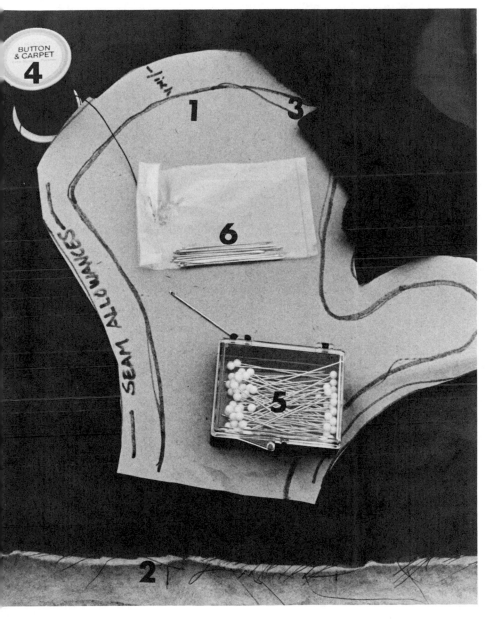

Materials: To make this project, you will need two to four furskins, about the size of a medium rabbit skin, depending on the size of the mittens and the size and usability of the pelts. The furs do not have to match or be in prime condition since the fur part will be the lining of the mitten. In fact, this is a good project for extra pelts, the ones that are not good enough for other garments or that don't match anything else in color and texture.

You will also need about a foot of forty-five-inch ski-jacket or other material for the outside of the mittens. Fabric that is quilted and waterproof will be warmer and longer wearing.

Also, you will need thread and a set of wristbands (knitted cuffs sold in sets in sewing supply stores for use on jackets and mittens) that match the color of the ski-jacket material. Any color of thread can be used on the fur lining. A glovers' needle is required for hand sewing and a medium needle for machine stitching (size #16-19) will work for both the fur and fabric.

Before you cut or even mark the pattern on the skins or ski-jacket material, make a muslin dummy using your hand pattern. Make sure that the fit is roomy enough without being too loose and that the opening is wide enough. Adjust your pattern if needed.

Tanned rabbit pelts.

*Fur lining and ski-jacket fabric mitten pieces
pinned together for sewing. Note how the seams
of the fur pieces are marked at intervals to
assure even matching.*

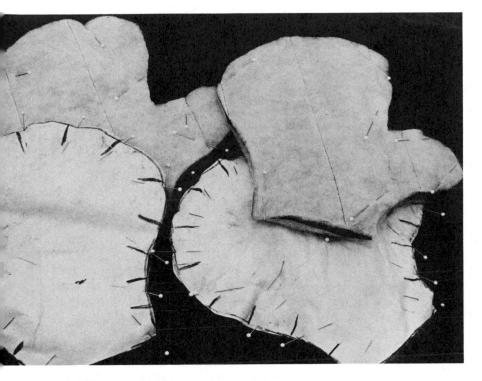

Assembly: Mark and cut the pattern from the furskins. Be sure you
make a right hand and a left hand by cutting two pieces of the pattern
and then turning it over and cutting two more. Since there is no front or
back to these mittens, you won't need to be concerned with that.

Add ½ inch all around the pattern and cut from the ski-jacket
fabric. The fabric outer mitten must be larger so that the fur lining fits
inside. If you want, you can add to the seam allowance of the fabric
pattern pieces (up to ⅝-inch seam allowance), but it's not necessary. If
you allow a wider seam, it's best to trim it back to ¼ inch after sewing
to reduce bulk.

Clip or pin the fur pieces together. Mark the seams of both pieces
at one- to two-inch intervals with a felt-tip or wax marking pen. Sew up
the glove lining on the skin side by hand or machine.

Where to clip and reinforce the outer fabric seam.

Pin the ski-jacket material pieces together and sew them up from the wrong side by hand or machine. You may have to adjust the tension and stitch length when you switch from fur to fabric on the sewing machine. Clip the fabric seams at the point where the thumb joins the rest of the hand to avoid puckering when you turn the glove right side out. Since this is the highest stress area of the mitten, reinforce the seam by stitching again where you clipped. Then turn the outer shell right side out. The seam can be flattened on the right side with a warm iron if you desire.

To join the glove together, follow these steps:

1. Slip the fur linings into the ski-jacket outer sections. Check for fit and make any adjustments now, before adding the cuffs. Then separate the two sections again.

2. Attach the fur linings to each cuff by sewing the wrist end of the lining to both sections of the cuff as shown in the illustration. You can slip the cuff inside the fur mitten for easier sewing, if you desire. Hold the cuff and lining together with pins or clips. Ease in any fullness by compressing or stretching the furskin or cuff as you sew. This step is easier if you sew by hand, stitching from the skin side and overcasting the edges.

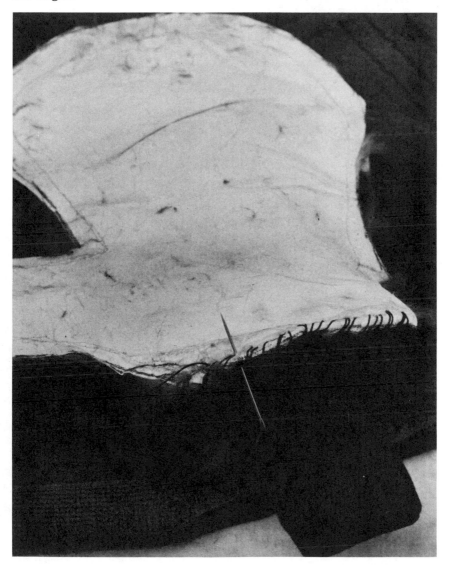

Attaching the fur lining to the knitted cuff.

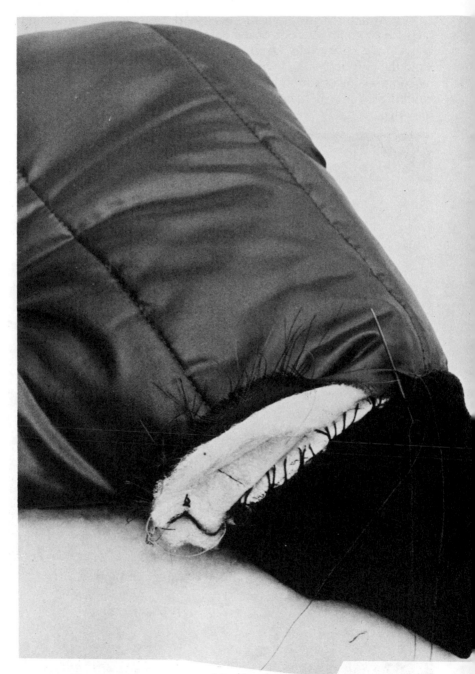

Attaching the outer mitten to the knitted cuff.

3. Slip the cuffed fur lining into the ski-jacket outer shell. Pin the outer mitten to the cuff, covering the fur seam line and turning the edge on the fabric toward the inside. Hand sew the fabric to the cuff, using an inconspicuous whipstitch, closely spaced for security and long wear.

The mittens are now ready to wear. If you want to make gloves with fingers or more complicated fitted mittens with set-in thumbs, patterns are available in several leatherworking books as well as fabric stores and crafts or leather outlets.

Completed mittens, showing the fur lining. A warmer pair of mittens you won't find!

Scraps

Fur scraps will accumulate faster than you can find uses for them if you do a lot of fur work. Here are several suggestions for your scraps:

Try piecing together square, rectangular, or odd-shaped pieces of similar weight, but different colors, for a fancy patchwork effect. When you get a sheet of scraps large enough, use it for lining mittens and slippers or for craft items.

Use the larger scraps to make small pouches, flaps for purses and jacket zippers, covered buttons, or novelties such as catnip-filled toys for cats.

Use the smaller scraps to stuff fur toys and pillows.

Sell or give the scraps to a craftsperson who makes fishing flies. They use the hair and fur bits to manufacture some really beautiful lures.

Dyeing Furs and Fur Garments

Commercially used furs are usually colored to achieve special effects or to match the color perfectly when several skins are needed to make a large garment. A special technique of the fur industry, called *blending*, involves dyeing the hair only, not the skin, to achieve an even color.

At home you can dye furs to match with a commercial hair dye, following the instructions on the package. A toothbrush or small paint brush can be used to achieve special effects or for dyeing only the tips of the fur.

Don't use hot or boiling water, which is often required with fabric dyes, to dye furs because the skin could dissolve to some extent.

Dry the dyed fur thoroughly and stretch to work out any stiff areas before cutting out the pattern pieces.

Mink Industry Methods

Furriers who construct those beautiful, expensive mink and chinchilla coats use techniques that are beyond the scope of this book and too difficult for the beginner to master anyway. One such technique is called *letting out*, also *dropping* or *stranding*. The mink or other small pelts are cut into long, diagonal strips; then these strips are reset and sewn together in a staggered formation to give the furrier a longer section of fur that is easier to work with. This technique improves the look of the fur by eliminating vertical lines that result when pelts are attached in patchwork squares, neck to rump.

Rabbit fur-lined footwear for chilly winter nights.

Rabbit fur bunnies are cuddly and soft.

Felt Manufacture from Rabbit Fur

Several years ago, the manufacture of felt was the major use for rabbit skins and fur. Today, most felt is synthetic and the only authentic fur felts are used for men's and women's hats.

To manufacture felt from fur, the guard hairs are removed and thrown away. Then the underfur is treated with chemicals (called *carrotting*) to assist the felting process and add strength, after which the skin is cut from the fur in strips. The resulting fur is blended and cleaned before being built up, layer by layer, and pressed against heated rollers to form felt.

Care and Cleaning of Fur Garments

Reduce the amount of cleaning and repair work your fur garment will need by treating it carefully during use and storage. Be especially careful about carrying shoulder bags with fur coats and jackets, as the constant rubbing will cause baldness at the shoulder.

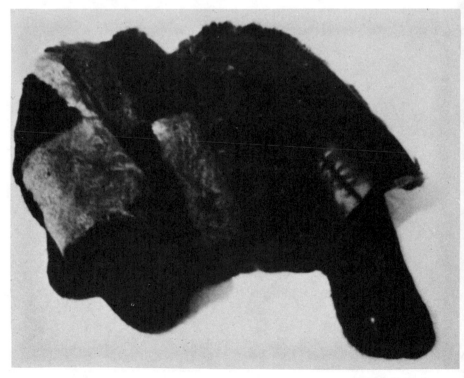

Rabbit fur jacket.

Never keep a fur in plastic. Use a fabric clothing bag to keep the dust from collecting on the garment. Store away from heat and light to lessen the danger of oxidation, a chemical action in the fur that causes a change, usually lightening, in the fur color.

If the fur needs overall cleaning, leave the job to a professional. Some commercial fur cleaners tumble the furs with nutshells or corn-meal before fluffing and brushing the hair.

To spot clean and remove the loose hair from fur garments, vacuum or brush the garment occasionally, or tumble in the dryer with no heat for a few minutes. Work or rub warm hardwood sawdust or dry cornmeal into the dirty spots. Shake off the excess and brush, beat, or vacuum out the remainder. Bran, powdered borax, chalk, or dry plaster of paris can also be used for spot cleaning in this manner.

If your fur item gets wet in the rain or snow, shake to remove most of the surface moisture, then hang it on a wooden or covered hanger and allow it to dry away from heat. When dry, brush, or fluff in an un-heated dryer.

When your fur garments and craft items are not being used, espe-cially during the summer, store in fabric clothing bags or boxes with mothballs or moth-repellent spray. Air them thoroughly before using them the next season.

Hanging furs in the sun and wind periodically helps deter insects. Or the entire garment can be soaked in borax water (¼ pound borax per gallon water) for an hour and hung up to air dry.

Sewing with fur is an enjoyable and often profitable handicraft. With a little practice and imagination, you can outfit your whole fam-ily in fur garments or earn a place of distinction at the local handicrafts shop.

Rabbit feet and tails before and after the bell caps are attached.

chapter 9

Basic Taxidermy

Taxidermy is the art of preparing and mounting animal skins in a lifelike manner. The taxidermist, a skilled person who skins, preserves, and mounts specimens usually in a commercial shop, studio, or a museum, is a scuptor, naturalist, artist, craftsperson, and wildlife anatomist as well as a tanner. His skill takes years to master—which is why it is such a challenging profession.

Most states require taxidermists to be licensed to practice commercially, but many people find it a rewarding, enjoyable hobby. True taxidermy began about 300 years ago as a hobby of the very rich.

Emphasis in taxidermy is on care and creating a natural-looking display rather than on speed. Many jobs takes months to get the project right. The following are the basic steps to preparing and mounting a life-size animal:

1. The animal is gutted and skinned with the fur or feathers kept carefully intact.

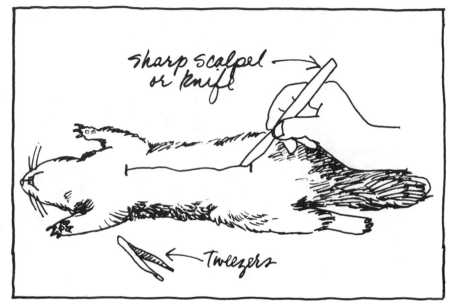

2. The animal skin is preserved or tanned.

3. The hide is mounted on a form made of straw, papier-mache, or wire.

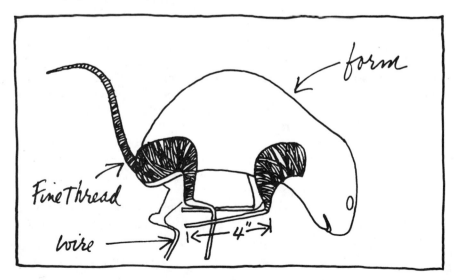

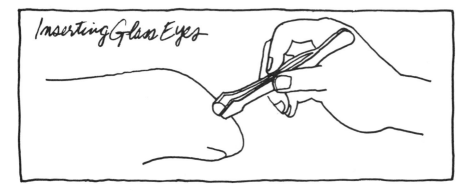

Inserting Glass Eyes

4. The specimen is worked into a lifelike position.

5. The finishing touches, glass eyes, teeth, other facial features, horns, and claws, are added.

The process is not as easy as this makes it seem. Further, several special tools are required to complete the job. If you are interested in taking up taxidermy as a profession or a hobby, I highly recommend that you read one or more of the excellent books on this subject listed in the Appendix. Visiting a taxidermist to see how it's done and what can be created is an enlightening experience as well.

Novelty Taxidermy

This is a branch of taxidermy concerned with the preservation and mounting of antlers, leathers, and skins (usually as wall hangings), and feet and tails.

Using otherwise-discarded feet and tails from fur-bearing animals can be an enjoyable hobby as well as a profitable craft. Every fur-bearer has four feet and a tail that can be made into charms to use on keyrings, hatbands, and as lucky pieces. Furthermore, the process is not difficult, and the materials are usually easily obtainable.

Many taxidermists preserve small mammals, amphibians, and reptiles in their entirety in 75 percent (150 proof) alcohol. I have found that alcohol is the best, easiest preservative for feet and tails, too. The alcohol solution penetrates easily and quickly in a few hours to a few days. However, the feet can be left in this solution for many weeks or months without damage. Tanning solutions cannot penetrate fast enough when bone and tissue are remaining in the feet and tails and often the fur will slip. Simple drying of these extremities does not work, either, because insects will destroy the dried foot or tail in short order without an insect repellent or preservative added.

To make charms from feet and tails, follow these steps:

1. Remove the feet and tail carefully from the animal. Cut off any excess tissue, ligaments, or skin but leave the foot or tail intact.

2. On large hind feet, you may wish to cut the foot in half with a sharp meat cleaver before preserving.

3. Wash the feet and tails in cold water to cool them and to remove any dirt. Use a mild soap solution if the feet are badly stained. Rinse well.

4. Immerse the feet and tails in 75 percent denatured alcohol. Soak in the solution at least forty-eight hours.

5. Squeeze out excess alcohol as you remove the feet and tails. The alcohol can be used again.

6. Rinse in a borax-water solution. Use about one cup of borax per gallon of water.

7. Rinse in plain water, squeeze out the excess, and lay out to dry, preferably in a warm room.

8. If you want to assure that no insects will damage the feet and tails later, work them through a bucket or bowl of dry borax.

9. Locate some bell caps for small feet novelties from the taxidermy supply dealer or a craft store. Attach a ring to the bell cap for use on key chains.

10. Place the bell cap over the bone end of the foot or tail. Pinch the bell cap all around for a snug fit. Remove the cap.

11. Use a good quality craft glue or contact cement to attach the cap to the foot or tail. Spread the glue evenly on both the bone end of the foot and around the inside of the bell cap. Allow the glue to dry a few minutes until just tacky, then put the two pieces together.

The caps can also be sewn to the feet with button and carpet or nylon thread. Some caps are available specifically for use with feet charms. These have sharp prongs that pierce into the foot and hold the cap in place. For security, these should be glued as well.

Taxidermists make a variety of crafts such as lamps, bookends, and gun racks from deer and other large animal feet. For supplies and information, contact a taxidermy supply dealer.

Fur Rugs

One of the most popular projects for many taxidermists is a fur rug made from a larger skin such as bear, wildcat, or coyote. A rug, complete with facial features and claws, lends any room a rustic effect and is eyecatching without being expensive.

Virtually any skin or section of skin in average or better than average condition can be used for rugs, wall hangings, throws, or auto seat covers. Felt borders are often added to blend in with any furnishings, and the hide is frequently lined to provide increased durability.

When skinning an animal for use as a rug, you must decide whether you want to use the feet and head or cut them off. It's far easier to cut them off, but many of the most exciting rugs include feet, claws, and facial features. If you are interested in using the feet and head, refer to one of the taxidermy books listed at the end of this book for complete instructions. The directions included in this book assume that you are using a hide minus the head and feet or a patchwork of several skins sewn together to rug size.

When skinning the animal, be careful to avoid irregular cuts. Then tan, soften, and finish the hide as directed in Chapter 3.

Use a shoe polish or hair dye in the nearest color to fill in light, bare areas in the hair or fur caused by scars, rubbed areas, or nipples.

Obtain a table or piece of plywood large enough to lay the skin out flat. This table must be something you can nail into.

Put the tanned, dry skin on the table, fur side down. Sponge warm borax-water (1 cup borax per gallon of water) over the entire flesh side until it is damp and relaxed.

Stretch the hide out as flat as possible with the fewest wrinkles. Nail each foot and the tail to the table to hold the hide in place. Nail the corners of a patchwork rug.

Sewing Wedges

Work on Skin side

Overcast Whip Stitch

Wedging and evening the rug skin.

Wedging: To make The Rug lie flat

Measure & mark darts from Center line for Symmetry

darts

darts: Triangles of skin cut out & sewn

work on skin side

center line

When working with an entire hide, the skin will undoubtedly bulge around the legs and near the neck. Hence, you will probably have to wedge or dart these areas to make the skin lie perfectly flat as shown in the illustration.

When the skin is lying flat, tack it down every few inches around the outside edge.

To trim the hide evenly, mark parallel lines on the skin in all directions using a yardstick and starting with the centerline down the middle of the back to form large squares.

Trim off the excess hide with a sharp knife or razor blade, and avoid cutting hairs. Leave the skin tacked down until completely dry.

Most fur rugs usually have two felt borders with pinked or scalloped edges. Bush-tailed, long-haired animals and woolskins are not usually bordered. Neither are patchwork rugs.

Positioning the felt borders on the skin.

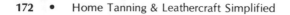

Border #1
1/2" wide

Border #2
1 1/2" wide

Clipping
to fit
Curves

Gathering
to fit
Curves

Fold under approximately 1"
Clip & Gather around Curves

Lining

Border #2

Attaching the lining to the rug.

When a double border is used, the colors are usually a pleasing combination such as red and black or brown and gold. Felt strips are available, precut, from taxidermy supply houses, or you can cut your own with a pinking or scalloping scissors.

Slip the first border under the section of skin to be bordered and position it to extend about ½ inch beyond the skin. Clip, staple, or glue it in place. The border will be more secure if you also sew it in place, using a strong thread that matches the fur color, not the border. Use a curved leather needle for easier sewing. Clip or gather felt at curves to lie flat.

Position the second border so that it extends ½ inch beyond the first and attach it in the same manner, again matching the thread to the fur.

Padding between the skin and the lining is optional, but often improves the durability of the rug. If it is used, stitch it to the skin in a few places to hold it securely while sewing on the lining.

An underlining of strong, good-quality felt, canvas, or flannel is used on all rugs. You will need a piece of fabric as large as the skin plus a one-inch folding edge all around.

Fold the lining edge under, leaving about one inch of felt showing underneath. Pin the lining to the felt. Sew the liner to the skin by stitching through all the thicknesses of felt as well as the skin, all around the hide. Use a small, closely-spaced stitch and thread to match the lining to be inconspicuous.

To speed the project, the bottom lining can be a layer of felt that extends all the way under the rug and beyond the first border, or the felt lining can be used to extend as the only border. Stitch in place and scallop the edges.

Comb the hair on the rug, especially around the outside edges. The rug is now ready for a proud position in your den.

Your rug will occasionally need to be vacuumed or shaken to remove loose dirt and hair. If the hide or the lining needs deeper cleaning, the stitching must be removed and the skin separated from the underliner. Although the liner can be washed by hand or machine, the hide should be cleaned by a professional. Adding new felt borders and/or lining to a cleaned fur rug will make it look almost new again and ready for a second life in your home or office.

appendix

Glossary

Alum—A white, astringent substance that shrinks skin fibers. The most common alum form is ammonium or potash alum. Several similar double sulphates are called "alum." SEE Chrome alum, aluminum sulphate.

Aluminum Sulphate—Potash alum's actual tanning substance. Chemical formula $Al_2(SO_4)18H_2$.

Angora Fur—The "wool" of certain species of rabbits and other animals that is spun for yarn.

Anthrax—A disease of cattle, sheep, and other animals. Contracted by contact with infected animals, carcasses, or hides. Symptoms include skin ulcers and lymph gland swelling.

Bark Tanning—SEE Oak Tanning.

Bating—Removing lime from a hide (neutralizing) by soaking in an acid. Used commercially, it means enzymes are added to remove hair roots and give a clean grain surface.

Beaming—Working tanned hides and skins over a tapered, rounded support to make them pliable and soft.

Bend—Lower back and rump section of a leather hide.

Beveling—Thinning leather edges by shaving.

Blending—Dyeing the ends (tips) or hair of the fur, but not the skin, to even or enhance the color.

Blue State—The condition of hides tanned with chrome alum that have a bluish-green coloring unless dyed.

Borax—White, crystalline salt frequently used for laundry.

Breaking the Skin—Stretching and working partly dried hides until they remain soft and supple.

Brucellosis (Bang's Disease)—A disease of cows, pigs, goats, and other animals. Contracted by contact with infected animals, carcasses, and hides. Symptoms include chronic or acute headache, fatigue, and chills.

Bubonic Plague—A plague transmitted by fleas from infected rodents. Symptoms include sudden onset of fever, chills, pain, and vomiting.

Buckskin—Soft, strong leather generally made from deerskin.

Carcass—Dead animal body.

Carrotting—Treating fur with chemicals to add strength and assist felting.

Cased Pelt—A pelt skinned with no lengthwise cut, fur in and flesh side out.

Chamois—Product of oil tanning the underneath layer that has been split from sheepskin.

Chrome Alum—Dark, glossy, plum-colored crystals. Basic chromium sulphate, chromium potassium sulphate, sodium carbonate, or bichromate potash. Chromium potassium sulphate crystals have the chemical formula $K_2SO_4Cr_2(SO_4)_3 24H_2O$.

Chrome Retan—Chrome tanning followed by vegetable tanning.

Chromium Potassium Sulphate—SEE Chrome Alum.

Chrome Tanned—Leathers tanned with soluble chromium salts, primarily basic chromium sulphate. Currently the most widely used tannage in USA.

Collagen—Main skin protein which is tanned. Forms a gelatin at high temperatures.

Corium—Network of collagen cells in the skin.

Crop—Section of leather hide including back, rump, and head but excluding the belly.

Curing—Applying salt to a green hide and allowing it to penetrate.

Currier's Knife—A tool that holds two very sharp, replaceable blades with turned edges for shaving down heavy hides and for fleshing.

Currying—Applying grease to leather or giving it a desirable finish. Also a term used for skiving or shaving a hide's thickness.

Damping Back—Moistening dry skin after tanning to render it pliable.

Denatured Alcohol—Grain alcohol rendered unfit for human consumption.

Depilatory—Hair, fur, or wool-removing substance.

Derma/Dermis—The true skin, the part from which leather is made.

Distemper—Viral disease of dogs, cats, and many wild animals. One type infects cats, another dogs. Raccoons, skunks, and mink can carry both kinds. Almost 100 percent fatal in both wild and domestic animals. Not transmissible to humans.

Doeskin—Sheep or lamb skins with hair removed.

Drenching—Removing or neutralizing hides after dehairing in lime by soaking in a weak acid solution.

Drumming—Tumbling hides and skins in an apparatus to aid cleaning, tanning, or stuffing. Removes excess oil and grease after tanning.

Dry-Milling—Tumbling previously dried leather in a large drum for thirty minutes to eight hours until softness desired is obtained.

Dry-Salted—A hide that has been salted and allowed to dry for one to two weeks. The dried skin is approximately two-thirds the weight of a green hide.

Dubbin—Mixture of equal parts grease and oil, warmed.

Electrolyte—Dilute sulphuric acid; battery acid.

Elongation—How far a material can stretch without breaking.

Epidermis—The external layer of skin that holds the hair.

Equilibrium Moisture—Ten to twelve percent moisture content in the skin, when the skin can be most easily stretched and softened.

Fat liquoring—Lubricating fibers with oils and related fatty substances so that after drying, they slide over one another. Regulates the leather's pliability, contributes to tensile strength, and has a bearing on how soft or firm the leather will be.

Fell—The thin membrane that lies between the meat (carcass) and the skin (hide).

Findings—Garment closures.

Fitch—Fur trade name for polecat or ferret.

Flaying—Skinning, especially furbearers.

Fleshing—Removing fat, flesh, tissue, and gristle from hide or skin.

Flint Hide—A hide dried without salting. It is half the weight of a green hide.

Full-Furred—Pelt in prime condition with well-developed guard hairs and underfur.

Fur Blending—Fur industry technique of dyeing the ends and hair of fur only, not the skin.

Fur Nap—The direction the fur grows (neck to rump).

Furrier—Person who sews with tanned furskins.

Glossy—An entire thickness of hide or the upper part of a split cowhide.

Glovers' Needle—Three-sided leather needle for soft leathers, suedes, and furs.

Grading—Separating hides or furs in a tannery according to quality.

Grain—The portion of hide on the hair side just under the epidermis.

Graining—Removing the hair and upper skin from hides to be made into leather.

Green Hide—A hide fresh off the animal carcass, cooled.

Green Salted—Description of a hide that is salted only, not dried. It is five-sixth the weight of a green hide.

Grutzen—Center back line of furskin, usually referring to mink.

Guard Hairs—Top covering of lusterous hair protecting the underfur.

Hairslip—Bacterial decay in the upper skin layers causing the fur to pull or "slip" off the skin in clumps.

Harness Needle—Dull-pointed needle for prepunched sewing holes in thick leather.

Hides—Large, heavy, thick skins from mature cattle and horses.

Keeper—Loop of leather to hold down the point of a belt after it has passed through the buckle.

Kips—Thin, supple skins, often with the hair left on after tanning, from calves, goats, sheep, and deer.

Last—Wooden or plastic idealized mold or form shaped like the human foot, used for making shoes.

Latigo—Oil-tanned cowhide or a type of retanned cowhide.

Leather Needle—A needle that has three sharp cutting knife edges at the point. Produces a cleaner hole in leather, and is easy to use.

Letting Out (Dropping, Stranding)—Mink industry technique of cutting pelts into diagonal strips and attaching the strips in a staggered formation.

Leptospirosis—General term for various diseases of farm livestock, skunks, cats, and other animals. Symptoms like influenza, but can affect the kidneys and become extremely severe.

Mange—A disease of wild and domestic animals caused by a microscopic mite that burrows tunnels through the skin of the host animal. Very contagious. Self-limiting to humans, but may cause red, itching welts on a person after handling infected animals.

Membrane—A very thin skin layer.

Mineral Tanning—(tawing, fur dressing) Alum or acid formulas.

Molt—Hair or skin shedding and regrowth.

Muslin Dummy—Sample garment made with inexpensive material to check size and fit of a pattern.

Naphthalene—Insect repellent used in a way similar to moth balls.

Neat's-Foot Oil—Pale yellow oil produced by boiling the feet and bones of "neat" cattle. The oil skimmed during glue-making when hooves and hide trimmings are boiled down in water. Used as a leather dressing.

Oak Tanning—Using an infusion of oak, hemlock, or other tannin-containing barks to preserve animal hides.

Oil of Vitrol—Sulphuric acid.

Oxidation—Chemical action in fur resulting in the change of fur colors.

Pasting—Fixing wet skins to a horizontal surface with a slicker and peeling them off when almost dry.

Peccary—South American hog. Source of pigskin for shoes, gloves, wallets, and luggage.

Pelt—Animal skins from furbearers.

Pickling—Treating hides and skins with salt and sulphuric acid. Preserving in alcohol.

Plates—Large sheets of fur made by sewing together squared pelts

Potash Alum—Chemical formula $K_2SO_4Al_2(SO_4)_324H_2O$. SEE Aluminum Sulphate.

Rabies—A virus disease that infects warm-blooded animals. Transmitted by bite or by saliva contact with a cut or scratch. An infected person is likely to die once the symptoms appear.

Ranch Mink—A standard dark brown color first developed on ranches.

Rawhide—Dehaired, untanned animal skin, stretched and dry cured.

Rex Fur—A mutant rabbit fur type that is ½ inch long, plush, dense, and very soft.

Ringworm—Skin infection of many domestic and wild animals. Transmitted by contact with infected animals, bedding, and skins. Affects hair, skin, and nails. Characterized by round, itching, reddened rings on the skin.

Rivet—Permanent two-part fastening used with leather.

Rocky Mountain Spotted Fever—An acute disease transmitted by ticks from infected rodents and other animals. Symptoms like influenza appear three to seven days after infection. Sensitivity to light is common. Can be fatal.

Rumping—Removing the hide from the buttocks of an animal during skinning.

Samming—Partly drying hides after tanning and before softening.

Scar-Dodging—Cutting patterns carefully from a leather hide to conserve material while avoiding blemishes.

Scores—Cuts and notches caused by careless skinning or fleshing. Cause flaws and blemishes in the finished leather.

Scudding—Working liquids, grease, or dirt out of skins by pressure and scraping. Using a slicker on the grain side of a skin.

Semi-Chrome Leather—Leather that has been vegetable tanned followed by chrome tanning.

Setting Out—Multi-purpose tanning operation that smooths and stretches the skin while squeezing out excess moisture and oil. Accomplished with a slicker.

Shearling—A skin that is suede on one side, wool, trimmed to an even thickness, on the other.

Shrinkage Temperature—Temperature of water at which a hide will shrink and shrivel. Increases as tanning material is absorbed by the skin.

Sides—Hide halves, usually cut down the center of the back.

Siding—Loosening the hide from the carcass with a sharp skinning knife starting at the split from the throat to tail and working out from the belly to the sides to the back. Cutting a large hide, such as a steer, in half along the backbone line.

Skiving—Thinning leather by shaving the edges of the back side.

Sleeking—SEE Scudding.

Sleeve-Pulled Pelt—SEE Cased Pelt.

Slicker—Wooden wedge, about six inches long, fitted to the palm of the hand and used for slicking, sleeking, scudding, and setting out.

Slicking—Smoothing with a wooden wedge to eliminate wrinkles from the leather surface. Also removes excess water or oil.

Staking—Working a tanned hide over a stake in the ground or with a rack and tools to soften and add flexibility by relaxing the skin fibers. Damp skin is pulled and stretched over a smooth, rigid surface on the flesh side to relax the fibers and soften the skin.

Sticking—Cutting an animal's throat to allow for complete blood drainage after killing but before skinning and butchering.

Stuffing—Working dubbin or oil into leather after tanning. Soaking hides in hot oil or wax.

Suede—Leather with a fuzzy nap on one or both sides.

Sulfonated (Oil)—Oil that is treated with sulfonic acid and is partly water-soluble.

Swivel Knife—An instrument used to cut leather patterns.

Taint—SEE Hairslip.

Tannery Run (TR) Hides—Ungraded tannery leather.

Tannic Acid—Active part of many vegetable materials with the ability to convert hide to leather.

Tannin—SEE Tannic Acid.

Tanning—Traditionally, treating with tannic acid solutions.

Taxidermy—The art of preparing and mounting animal skins in a lifelike manner.

Tawing—Treating skins with aluminum compounds.

Temper—Varying degrees of softness.

Tensile Strength—The greatest longitudinal stress a substance can bear without tearing apart, measured in pounds per square inch.

Thonging Punch—A tool used to punch sewing holes in leather.

Toggling—Drying a wet pelt in a stretched position by using clips called toggles along the skin edges which attach to a frame.

Tooling—Leather carving with knives and stamps.

Tousing—Stretching, twisting, and working a tanned skin to produce pliability and softness. SEE Breaking the Skin.

Tramping—Forcing mixtures of oils and greases into skins by machine to protect further from rot and stiffness after tanning.

Tularemia—(Rabbit Fever) A disease of rodents and rabbits usually transmitted by direct contact. Symptoms like influenza. Can be fatal without treatment.

Vegetable Tanning—SEE Oak Tanning.

Washing Soda—Crystallized sodium carbonate. Clear, glasslike crystals.

Suggested Reading/Bibliography

Books and Pamphlets

ALL ABOUT MINK. EMBA Mink Breeders Association, Racine, WI.

Faye Arnim, *FUR CRAFT: HOW TO GLAMORIZE YOUR WARDROBE WITH FUR* (Key Books).

CHINCHILLA RAISING. (Morrison, CO: Empress Chinchilla Breeders Cooperative, 1967).

Maurice H. Decker, *PRACTICAL HOME TANNING AND FUR DRESSING* (St. Paul, MN: Webb Book Publishing Co., 1934, 1935, 1942).

EDUCATIONAL BROCHURE OF PRIMER TRAPPING. (Murray, KY: Fur Takers of America).

Albert B. Farnham, *HOME MANUFACTURE OF FURS AND SKINS* (Columbus, OH: A. R. Harding).

Albert B. Farnham, *HOME TANNING AND LEATHERMAKING GUIDE* (Columbus, OH, 1950).

Frey, et. al, *HOME TANNING* (Shorey, 1936).

Jane Garnes, *THE COMPLETE HANDBOOK OF LEATHERCRAFTING* (Blue Ridge Summit, PA: Tab Books, 1979).

Sylvia Grainger, *LEATHERWORK* (New York: J. B. Lippincott Co., 1976).

Gerald J. Grantz, *HOME BOOK OF TAXIDERMY AND TANNING* (Harrisburg, PA: Stackpole Books, 1969).

Elsie Hanauer, *CREATING WITH LEATHER* (San Diego, CA: A. S. Barnes, 1970).

William F. Happich, *HOME TANNING WOOLSKINS WITH GLUTARALDEHYDE* (Philadelphia, PA: Eastern Regional Research Laboratory of the U.S.D.A., 1968).

Larry Hemard, *LEATHERCRAFT: CREATIVE TECHNIQUE AND DESIGN* (Garden City, NY: Doubleday & Co., 1972).

HIDES AND SKINS. U.S. Hide, Skin and Leather Association, Washington, DC.

HIDES AND SKINS FROM LOCKER PLANTS AND FARMS. U.S.D.A. Publication #857. Washington, DC, 1961.

Richard L. Hiner, *SLAUGHTERING, CUTTING AND PROCESSING BEEF ON THE FARM U.S.D.A. Farmers Bulletin #2209.* Washington, DC.

Phyllis Hobson, *TAN YOUR HIDE!* (Charlotte, VT: Garden Way Publishing, 1977).

Lloyd & Audrey Kempf and Van Dyke, *TANNING* (Woonsocket, RI: Van Dyke Supply Co., 1971).

Lloyd & Audrey Kempf et al, *RUGMAKING* (Woonsocket, RI: Van Dyke Supply Co., 1971, 1980).

Sid Latham, *LEATHERCRAFT* (Chicago: Follett, 1978).

LEATHERFACTS. New England Tanners Club, Peabody, MA, 1965.

LEATHER IN OUR LIVES: THE STORY OF AMERICAN LEATHER. Leather Industries of America, New York, NY.

Otis Mason, *ABORIGINAL SKIN DRESSING.* Smithsonian Annual Report, 1889. Facsimile Reproduction, 1971.

Waddy F. McFall, *TAXIDERMY STEP BY STEP.* (Piscataway, NJ: Winchester Press, 1975).

Brenda Mills, *MADE IN SUEDE: THE ART OF TAILORING IN SOFT LEATHER.* Transatlantic.

Mary A. Patton, *DESIGNING WITH LEATHER AND FUR (REAL AND FAKE).* Hearthside, 1972.

Grete Peterson, *LEATHERCRAFTING.* (New York, NY: Sterling Publishing Co., 1980).

Nadine H. Roberts, *THE COMPLETE HANDBOOK OF TAXIDERMY.* (Blue Ridge Summit, PA: Tab Books, 1980).

David and Inger Runk, *SHOES FOR FREE PEOPLE.* (Santa Cruz, CA: Unity Press, 1976).

Schwebke and Krohn, *HOW TO SEW LEATHER, SUEDE AND FUR.* (New York, NY: MacMillan, 1974).

SKIN, HIDE AND LEATHER DEFECTS. Tanners Council Research Laboratory, Cincinnati, OH.

Roberta Stark, *HOW TO TAN & SEW YOUR RABBIT FURS AT HOME.* (Issaquah, WA: Furreal Enterprises, 1982).

TRAPPING AND WILDLIFE MANAGEMENT. Woodstream Corp., Niagara Falls, Ontario, 1980.

June Vivian, *HOME TANNERS' HANDBOOK.* (London: A. H. & A. W. Reed, Ltd., 1976).

For More Information . . .

Chronical Guidance Publications, Inc., Moravia, NY 13118.
        Occupational Brief #142—*Shoe Industry Workers*
        Occupational Brief #211—*Fur Industry Workers*
        Occupational Brief #297—*Leather Tanning & Finishing Workers*
        Occupational Brief #334—*Leatherworker*
        Occupational Brief #512—*Taxidermist*

Empress Chinchilla, P.O. Box 402, Morrison, CO 80465   (303) 697-4421

Fur Takers of America, Earl Allen, business manager.
        Route 6, Box 210-A., Murray, KY 42071

National Board of Fur Farm Organizations,
        450 N. Sunnyslope Rd., Suite 120,
        Brookefield, WI 53005
        (414) 786-4242

National Trappers Assoc., Inc.
        15412 Tau Rd.
        Marshall, MI 49068

New England Tanners Club
        Box 371
        Peabody, MA 01960

Science Research Associates. 259 E. Erie St., Chicago, IL 60611
        Occupational Brief #45—*Fur Farmers*
        Occupational Brief #176—*Leather Manufacturing Workers*

Tanners' Council of America, Inc.
    2501 M St. NW
    Washington, DC 20037
    (202) 785-9400
    Membership Directory: Tanneries, Suppliers, Manufacturers (free)

U.S. Hide, Skin and Leather Association
    1707 N St. NW
    Washington, DC 20036

Fur Buyers

B & B Fur Buyers
Phoenix, AZ 85021

BECA, Inc. (raw furs)
Route 1, Box 2
Highway 12 East
Sturgis, MS 39769

Blue Diamond Fur Ranch
14630 Badger Pass Rd.
Morgan Hill, CA 95037

Feles Presburger
10501 Wilshire Blvd., Suite 904
Los Angeles, CA 90024

4D Rabbit Farm & Fur Co.
Drawer #288
Huntington, TX 75649
Attention: Alvin E. Dominey

H. E. Goldberg Co.
Seattle, WA

Grand River Fur Exchange
6310 U.S. 6
Rome, OH 44085

Gunter Fur & Rabbit Products
19411 SE Greenvalley Rd.
Auburn, WA 98002

Mills
Box 95
Numidia, PA 17858

Moe Lipson Co., Inc.
143 W. 30th St.
New York, NY 10001

Moscow Hide & Fur
Box 8918
Moscow, ID 93943

River Ranch
Route 1, Box 157
Pendleton, OR 97801

Val & Era's
570 S. Linder Rd.
Meridian, ID 83642

Leather and Fur Sellers

For local leather and fur dealers, look in the phone book Yellow Pages under the following listings: Leather, Fur, Tanners, Livestock Dealers, Leather Clothing—Retail, Leather Goods—Dealers, Fur Business—Retail, Fur Business—Wholesale & Manufacturers, Meat Packers.

American Fur Dressing, Inc.
10816 Newport Highway
Spokane, WA 99218

Berman Leathercraft
25 Melchor
Boston, MA 02210

Century Leather Co., Inc.
110 Beach St.,
Boston, MA 02111

Cleveland Leather Co.
2824 Lorain Ave.
Cleveland, OH 44113

D'Narb Ltd.
100 Myrtle Ave.
Havertown, PA 19083

Double D Leather Co.
6212 D Madison Pike
Huntsville, AL 35806

Drake Leather Co., Inc.
3500 W. Beverly Blvd.
Montebello, CA 90640

Funk & Rose
212 S. 15th Ave.
Minneapolis, MN 55404

Leather
19 E. Woodside Ave.
Ardmore, PA 19003

Leather Crafters' Supply Co.
25 E. 3rd St.
New York, NY 10012

Leather, Etc.
2033 University Ave.
Berkeley, CA 94704

Leather Unlimited Co.
P.O. Box 23002
Milwaukee, WI 53223

Leon Leather Co., Inc.
1738 E. 2nd St.
Scotch Plains, NJ 07076

Mac Leather Co.
424 Broome St.
New York, NY 10013

Montana Leather Co.
Doug Mac Pherson
2015 1st Ave. North
P.O. Box 394
Billings, MT 59103
406-782-4743

Monroe Fur & Leather, Ltd.
5087 Ridge Rd. West
Spencerport, NY 14559

Richmond Leather Co.
1839 W. Broad St.
Richmond, VA 23220

Southwestern Leather & Shoe Findings Co.
27 N. 3rd St.
Box 3555
Phoenix, AZ 85030

Tandy Leather Company
Headquarters: Forth Worth, TX
Local outlet listed in phone book
Yellow Pages under Leather

Tanners' Council of America, Inc.
2501 M St. NW
Washington, DC 20037
—Directory of tanneries and sellers

Worth Leather Co.
151 Allen Blvd.
Farmingdale, NY 11735

Suppliers

Alice Brooks
NeedleCraft Dept.
Box 167—Old Chelsea Station
New York, NY 10113
—Catalog available
—Patterns for garments and crafts

Amber Leather Co.
835 San Julian
Los Angeles, CA 90052
—Leatherwork supplies

American Fur Dressing, Inc.
10816 Newport Highway
Spokane, WA 99218
—Tanning services

Artistic Taxidermy
18607 St. Claire Ave.
Cleveland, OH 44110
—Taxidermy & Tanning supplies & services

Aulson Tanning Machinery Co.
50 Rantoul St.
P.O. Box 491
Beverley, MA 01915

BECA, Inc.
Route 1, Box 2, Highway 12 East
Sturgis, MS 39769
—Fur dressing and tanning services
—Traps & trapping supplies

Berman Leathercraft
25 Melchor
Boston, MA 02210
—Catalog available
—Leatherworking supplies

Bob's Taxidermy Supply
321 N. Perry St.
Johnstown, NY 12095
—Supplies and services

Bucks County Fur Products, Inc.
P.O. Box 204
Quakertown, PA 18951
—Taxidermy and tanning services

Cedar Lake Trapping Supply
1221 University Blvd.
Richmond, IN 47374
—Catalog available

Century Leather Co., Inc.
110 Beach St.
Boston, MA 02111
—Catalog available
—Leatherworking supplies

Cleveland Leather Co.
2824 Lorain Ave.
Cleveland, OH 44113
—Catalog available
—Leatherworking supplies

Colorado Tanning Co.
1787-93 S. Broadway
Denver, CO 80210
—Taxidermy and tanning services

Commonwealth Felt Co.
211 Congress St.
Boston, MA 02110
—Felt rug lining and borders

Continental Felt Co.
22 West 15th St.
New York, NY 10011
—Felt rug lining and borders

Drake Leather Co., Inc.
3500 W. Beverly Blvd.
Montebello, CA 90640
—Catalog available
—Leatherworking supplies

Elwood Supply Co.
Box 3507
Omaha, NE 68103
—Tanning & fleshing knives

Furreal Enterprises
P.O. Box 1101
Issaquah, WA 98027
—Catalog available
—Rabbit fur patterns

GAF Corp. Chemical Products
140 W. 51st St.
New York, NY 10020
—Tanning chemicals

J. E. Trodden & Co.
257 Randolph St.
Napa, CA 94558
—Tanning services

J. G. Read & Bros. Co., Inc.
101-21st St., Box 469
Ogden, UT 84402
—Catalog available
—Leatherworking supplies

Leather's Best, Inc.
30 Hub Drive
Melville, NY 11747
—Tanning services

Leather Unlimited Co.
P.O. Box 23002
Milwaukee, WI 53223
—Catalog available
—Leatherworking supplies

Leathercrafters' Supply Co.
25 E. 3rd St.
New York, NY 10012
—Catalog available

Leon Leather Co., Inc.
1738 E. 2nd St.
Scotch Plains, NJ 07076
—Catalog available
—Leatherworking supplies

Macpherson Leather Supply
P.O. Box 882783
San Francisco, CA 94188-2783
(415) 285-3306
—Catalog available
—Leatherworking supplies

Meyer Brand Trapline Products
Box 153
Garrison, IA 52229
—Fur stretchers
—Traps

Monroe Fur and Leather, Ltd.
5087 Ridge Rd. West
Spencerport, NY 14559
—Tanning services

Moscow Hide and Fur
Box 8918
Moscow, ID 83843
—Catalog available
—Trapping supplies

Napa Custom Tanning
1090 Revere
San Francisco, CA 94124
—Chrome tanning services

Northwoods Wildlife Mgmt. Equipment
Box 375
Greensburg, PA 15601
—Trapping supplies

Pioneer Trap Mfg., Inc.
2909 NE Alberta
Portland, OR 97211
—Trapping supplies

Princeton Process, Inc.
501 S. Main St.
Spring City, PA 19475
—Chinchilla dressing & marketing

Richmond Leather Co.
1839 W. Broad St.
Richmond, VA 23220
—Catalog available
—Leatherworking supplies

Rittel's
170 Dean Street
Taunton, MA 02780
—Catalog available
—Tanning chemicals & supplies

Rochester Fur Dressing Co., Inc.
219 Smith St.
Rochester, NY 10001
—Taxidermy and tanning services

Southeastern Outdoor Supplies, Inc.
Route 3, Box 503
Bassett, VA 24055
—Catalog available
—Hunting and trapping supplies

Stan Krofick Trapping Supplies
RD 2, Box 83
Latrobe, PA 15650

Sullivan Fur Dressing, Inc.
Box D
Oakhurst, CA 93644
—Fur dressing services

TAC Tannins & Chemicals, Inc.
30 Montgomery St.
Jersey City, NJ 07300
—Vegetable tanning extracts

Tandy Leather Company
Advertising Department
P.O. Box 791
Fort Worth, TX 76101
—Catalog available
—Leather, fur, patterns,
    leatherworking supplies

Tanners' Council of America, Inc.
2501 M St. NW
Washington, DC 20037
—Directory of suppliers: Tools,
    chemicals, and tanning services

The Tannery, Inc.
2012 E. Monroe
Riverton, WY 82501
—Tanning services

Turner Tanning Machinery
Elliot Street
Beverly, MA 01915

Union Carbide Chemical Co.
270 Park Ave.
New York, NY 11205
—Glutaraldehyde and other
    tanning chemicals

Van Dyke's
Woonsocket, SD 57385
—Catalog available
—"Everything for taxidermy &
    related crafts"

Worth Leather Co.
151 Allen Blvd.
Farmingdale, NY 11735
—Catalog available
—Leatherworking supplies

For local suppliers, check the following listings in the phone book Yellow Pages: Chemicals, Tanners, Leather, Butchers' Equipment & Supplies, Craft Supplies, Gift Shops, Fabric Shops, Sewing Machines—Household, Sewing Machines—Industrial & Commercial, Felt & Felt Products, Notions—wholesale & Manufacturers, Livestock Dealers.

For sewing patterns, check the local fabric shops in your area. Catalogs and patterns are available from Butterick, Simplicity, McCalls, Vogue, and others.

index

Numbers in italics refer to illustrations.

Aquatic animals • 24, 49

Alligator • 97

Alum • 42, 60–62

Alum-salt • 49, 60–63, 74

Alum-salt-soda • 62

Alum-washing soda • 88

B

Bag tanning • 87 and *illus.*

Baking powder • 58

Bating • 72

Bear • 30, 36, 170

Belt, leather • 131–137

Beveler • *120*, 123, 126, 132

Blue state • 75

Boddicker, Major L. • 25

Borax • 52, 59, 62, 70, 163, 170

Breaking the skin • 55–58, *56, 57*.
See *also* Softening leather

Brine curing • 38

Buckles • *120*, 131 and *illus.*

Butchering defects • 101

C

Calfskin • 75, 92, *104*, 128

Calves • 20, 29, 35

Carbolic acid • 89

Carrotting • 162

Cattle hides • 34, 36, 75, 108–109

Chamois • 109

Chinchilla • 18–19, 119, 141

Chrome alum • 75

Chrome tanning • 75–77

Corium • 106–107 and *illus.*

Cowhides • *See* Cattle hides

Curing • 36–37, 38

Curing room • 37

D

Deerskin • 29, 108

Dehairing • 71–72

Deliming • 72–73

Derma • 49, 51

Diseases • 14–15

Dog collar, leather • 131–137

Draining • *See* Sticking

Drench • *See* Bating

Dressing • 60

Drumming • 58, 63

Dry-milling • 81

Dry salted hides • *See* Hides, salt-hard

Dubbin • 74, 79, 80, 90

Dyeing furs • 160

Dyeing leather • 76, 78, 127, *134*

E

Equilibrium moisture • 53, 55, 58

F

Fat liquoring • 81

Fell • 35

Felt manufacture • 162

Finishing • 52, 58–59, 78–81

Fleshing • 49–51, *50*, 68–70, *69*

Fleshing beam • 68 and *illus.*, 78, 93

Fur garments,
  care and cleaning • 162–163

Fur rugs • 36, 170–173

Fur scraps • 160

Fur skins •

  brushing • 59 and *illus.*, *147*, 151

  cutting • 145–146

  degreasing • 26, 49

  freezing • 26, 61

  sewing • 148–151

  storage • 60, 103

  washing • 52

G

Garment leathers • 80–81.
  See also Leather, types of

Gasoline • 49, 62

Glue • 116 and *illus.*, 130

Glutaraldehyde tanning • 93–95

Goats • 20, 29, 36

Goat skins • 75, 108

Goldberg, Irwin • 22

Grain (epidermis) • 71, *107*

Grain (fur growth direction) • 145

Guard hairs • 22

H

Hairslip • 26, 39, 61, 62, *98*, 101–102, 147

Happich, William • 93

Hides •

  defects in • 99–101

  defined • 14

  flint • 38

  salt-hard • 37, 38, 61

  washing • 70

Hole punches • *120*, 122–123 and *illus.*, *133*

Holes, in fur skins • 147

I

Insect damage • 59, 60, 100

K

Keeper • 136 and *illus.*

Killing • 25, 30

Knives •

  currier's • 69, *70*

  fleshing • 69, *70*

  grapefruit • *50*, 51

  leather • 121, *122*, *123*, 146

  skinning • 26, *31*, 33, *70*

  skiving • 69, 123 and *illus.*

  swivel • 126

L

Lambs • 20

Lamb skin • 75

Last • 138

Latigo • 109

Leather •

 alum-tanned • 44

 amounts needed for projects • 124

 chrome-tanned • 44

 expanded • 124, *125*

 oak-tanned • 44, 127

 properties of • 106–107

 sewing • 112–119, 128–129

 tanning • 74–77

 thickness of • 109–111, *110*

 types of • 14, 108–109

Leather care • 139

Leather needles • 112

M

Mildew • 56

Mineral tanning • 88–89

Mink • 18, *19*, 22, 119, 141, 142

Mink industry methods • 160

Mink oil • 45, 59

Mittens, fur-lined • 152–159

Molting • 22, 101, 102

Muslin dummy • 111, 144

N

Neat's-foot oil • 45, 59, 62, 74, 78, 79, 81, 86, 89, 90, 92, 94, 139

Neutralizing rinses • 52, 64, 72, 76, 89

O

Oak-tanning • *See* Vegetable tanning

Oil tanning • 90

Oxalic acid • 88–89

P

Pasting • 55, 63

Patterns, cutting • 124–125, 144–146

Pelts •

 defined • 14

 cased (sleeve-pulled) • 27

 degreasing • 49

 full furred/prime • 17–20, 22–24, 141

 matching • 143

 salt-dried • 61

 washing • 47

Pigskin • 30, 108

Potash alum • 61

Pretanning • 74

Projects •

 leather belt • 131–137

 leather wristband • 131–137

 leather dog collar • 131–137

 fur-lined mittens • 152–158

R

Rabbit • 17, 22, *23*, 26, 49, 51, *104*, 119, *140*, 141, 142

Rawhide • 66, 73–74, 90, 109

Retanning • 88

Rivets • *120*, 130, 135

Rumping • 35

S

Saddle soap • 139

Scudding • 73, 86

Setting out • 78

Sewing • 112–119 and *illus.*, 128, 141–161, *148*

Sharkskin • 97, 108

Sheep • 20, 26, 29, *94–95*

Sheepskins • 36, 38–39, *39*, 49, 75, 87, 92–95, 108–109

Shoemaking • 138

Shrinkage temperature • 65

Siding • 34 and *illus.*

Skinning • 25–26, 30–32, *35*

Skins •

    cooling green • 26, 36, 102

    defined • 14

    degreasing green • 26

    handling green • 26, 36

    number needed for projects • 142

Skiver • *123*

Slicker • *70*, 73, 78, 79, 86

Snakeskin • 97–98

Softening leather • 78–81. *See also* Breaking the skin

Snaps • 130

Spray, wig conditioner • 60

Staking • 79–80, *80*

Stamping designs • 127 and *illus.*

Sticking • 33

Suede • 108–109, 139

Sulphuric acid • 42, 43, 63–65

T

Tannery run hides • 111

Tannic acid • 42

Tannin extraction • 84–87

Tan trough • 74

Tanning •

    chemicals • 42–43, *82*

    defined • 11, 42

    recipes • 60–65, 75–77, 84–86, 88–89, 90, 92, 93, 96–97

    room • 44

    tests • 65, 76, 85, 94

    tools • *70*

    See also individual processes

Tawing • *See* Sulphuric acid

Taxidermy • 165–173

Toggling • 55

Tooling • 126

Tools, for leatherwork • *120*, 121. *See also* individual tools

Tramping • 59

Trapping • 20–22, 25

V

Vegetable tanning • 83–87

W

Washing soda • 61

Water, hard • 42–43

Woolskins • *See* Sheepskins

Wristband, leather • 131–137